Go Beyond intro

STUDENT'S BOOK

Robert Campbell
Rob Metcalf
Rebecca Robb Benne

LISTENING & VOCABULARY ▶	GRAMMAR (2)	LANGUAGE & BEYOND	SPEAKING ▶	WRITING
It's a small world! **Listen to a description of where things are from** **Vocabulary (2):** Countries and nationalities	*This/that, these/those* **Talk about the things around you**	School skills **Be a good classmate**	Is it new? **Describe things**	My things (description) **Write a description of a thing**
Whose is it? **Listen to a quiz show** **Vocabulary (2):** Parts of the body	*Whose?*; possessive *'s/s'* and possessive pronouns **Talk about your things, family, and friends**	School skills **Be friendly to other students**	On the phone **Talk on the phone**	My favorite person (description) **Write a description of a person**
A new neighbor **Listen to a description of a room** **Vocabulary (2):** Things in your room	*There is / there are* **Describe a room**	School skills **Prepare your things for school**	You're welcome **Ask for and give things**	Don't forget (note) **Write a note**
Are you musical? **Listen to street interviews** **PRONOUNCE** The /v/ sound **Vocabulary (2):** Music	Simple present **Talk about habits and routines**	School skills **Write down your homework**	What time is it? **Tell the time**	My free time (email) **Write an email**

S STARTER GET READY: IT'S MY PARTY

HELLO!

Come to our costume party!
(Wear a costume with your favorite color.)
It's on Saturday at 4 o'clock.
We live at 20 Hill Street.
Come with a friend.
Ben and Karen

Number two … number four … six …

THINK AND READ

1 ▶1.01 Read the story. What's Emily's favorite color?

2 Read the story again and do the exercises.

RECALL

1 NUMBERS 1–20

a ▶1.02 Work in pairs. Complete the numbers with *a*, *e*, *i*, *o*, and *u*. Then listen and repeat.

1 *o* n *e*   6 s ___ x   11 ___ l ___ v ___ n   16 s ___ xt ___ ___ n
2 tw ___   7 s ___ v ___ n   12 tw ___ lv   17 s ___ v ___ nt ___ ___ n
3 thr ___   8 ___ ght   13 th ___ rt ___ ___ n   18 ___ ght ___ ___ n
4 f ___ r   9 n ___ n   14 f ___ ___ rt ___ ___ n   19 n ___ n ___ t ___ ___ n
5 f ___ v   10 t ___ n   15 f ___ ft ___ ___ n   20 tw ___ nty

b Work in pairs. Student A: say a number from 1 to 20. Student B: Close your book. Write the number in letters. Student A: Check the number. Then change roles.

2 INTRODUCTIONS

a Put the words in order to make sentences.

Maria: Hi. *Maria. / I'm*
Hi. (1) *I'm Maria.*
Eric: Hello. *Eric. / My / name's*
Hello. (2) _____
Maria: *is / This / Mark.*
(3) _____

b ▶1.03 Listen and check. Then listen and repeat.

3 PRONOUNS AND POSSESSIVE ADJECTIVES
Complete the table. Use words from the pictures.

(1) ___ *I'm* ___ Ben.	(2) ___ *My* ___ name's Ben.
You're Emily.	(3) _____ name's Emily.
(4) _____ 's Eric.	**His** name's Eric.
She's Karen.	**Her** name's Karen.
(5) _____ 's a house.	**Its** address is 20 Hill Street.
We're Ben and Karen.	(6) _____ names are Ben and Karen.
You're Emily and Eric.	**Your** names are Emily and Eric.
They're Lucy and Maria.	**Their** names are Lucy and Maria.

4 ▶1.04 Complete Karen's sentences with words from the table in Exercise 3. Then listen and check your answers.

1 "Lucy's here with ___her___ friend, Maria."
2 "This is Mark, and this is _____ brother."
3 "The pizzas? _____ 're on the table."
4 "Hi, Eric. _____ sunglasses are great!"
5 "The cat? It lives next door. _____ name is Star."

5 COLORS

▶1.05 Match the colors to the words in the box. Listen and repeat.

black	blue	brown	green	orange
pink	purple	red	white	yellow

6 BE

a Complete the sentences with *am*, *are*, or *is*.

Karen: They (1) ___are___ my friends from school. We (2) _____ in the same class.
Ben: Eric (3) _____ number 7 on the team, and I (4) _____ number 11.
Karen: His name (5) _____ Mark. You (6) _____ at the same school.
Ben: Kayla (7) _____ from Canada. Karen and Kayla (8) _____ really good friends.

b ▶1.06 Listen and check.

7 HAVE A PARTY

Write an invitation for your party. Use the invitation in the story to help you.

AT THE PARTY

1 Let's play games!

2 This game's Buzz. We count from 1 to 100, but for 5, 10, 15, 20, and so on, you say "Buzz."

5 OK, one more game. First, we say our birthday months. When I say "go," you stand in order, with January here.

My birthday's in June.

6 The food's ready!

THINK AND READ

1 ▶1.07 Read the story. Who's Maximus?

2 Read the story again and do the exercises.

RECALL

1 NUMBERS 20–100

▶1.08 Match the numbers to the words. Then listen and repeat.

20   30   40   50   60   — thirty   **twenty**   forty
70   80   90   100   — sixty   one hundred
                                    seventy   fifty   **ninety**
                              eighty

2 DAYS OF THE WEEK

a ▶1.09 Write the days of the week in order. Listen and check. Then listen and repeat.

| Friday | Saturday | Sunday |
| Thursday | Wednesday | |

Monday ....
Tuesday ....
....
....

b Work in pairs. Close your books. Write the days. Then check your spelling.

3 MONTHS

a Work in pairs. Write the months in order.

| April | August | December | ~~February~~ | March | May |
| ~~January~~ | July | June | October | September | November |

January, February, ...

b ▶1.10 Listen and check. Then listen and repeat.

4 *BE:* **NEGATIVE, QUESTIONS, AND SHORT ANSWERS**

▶1.11 Complete the conversation. Then listen and check.

| am | are | aren't | ~~is~~ | isn't | 'm not |

Leo: Hi. I'm Maximus.
Emily: (1) ___Is___ that your real name?
Leo: No, it (2) _____. And I (3) _____ really a gladiator.
Emily: (4) _____ you one of Ben's friends?
Leo: Yes, I (5) _____ , but we (6) _____ friends from school.

5 QUESTION WORDS

a Match the question words (1–5) to the pictures (a–e).

1 Who? _e_   4 When? _____
2 What? _____   5 How old? _____
3 Where? _____

b ▶1.12 Complete the conversation with question words. Then listen and check.

Emily: (1) _How old_ are you?
Leo: I'm 13.
Emily: (2) _____'s your birthday?
Leo: It's in October. And your birthday's in May.
Emily: That's right! (3) _____ are you?
Leo: I'm Maximus.
Emily: (4) _____'s your *real* name?

6 PHONE CONTACTS

Work in pairs. Complete the contact information for your partner.

What's your ... ?

How old ... ?

When's your ... ?

Name: _____
Phone number: _____
Age: _____
Birthday: _____
Address: _____

UNIT 1 ME

IN THE PICTURE My things

>>> Talk about your things

WORK WITH WORDS Things

1 Work in pairs. What things can you name in the pictures?

2 a Match the things in the pictures (1–15) to the words in the box.

> backpack bike car game console
> ice cream jeans laptop notebook
> orange phone sandwich soccer ball
> sunglasses T-shirt website

PHRASE BYTES

What's this?
It's a / an …
They're …
I don't know.

b ▶1.13 Listen and check your answers. Then listen and repeat.

3 a Work in pairs. Write the words in Exercise 2a in the best categories.

Clothes	Food	Games
School	Technology	Transportation

b Compare your answers with the rest of the class.

c ▶1.14 Listen and check your answers.

4 a Work in groups. Add other words to the categories.

b Which group has the most words for each category? Make a class list of all the words.

5 **THE MOVING PICTURE** ▶ Watch the video. Write the categories in the correct order.

6 a ▶1.15 **PRONOUNCE** Listen to the alphabet. Repeat the letters.

b Work in pairs. Student A: spell a word from this lesson. Student B: write it. Say "stop" when you know it.

> B – I – K …

> Stop! Is it "bike"?

> Yes, that's right. / No. Try again!

MY THINGS

WRITE AND SPEAK

7 🌐 **Work in pairs. Write your favorite word for each category in Exercise 3a. Then compare with your partner.**

PHRASE BYTES

What's your favorite word for food?

My favorite word is …

What's your word?

How do you say … in English?

MOVE BEYOND

Do the Words & Beyond exercise on page 106.

Workbook, page 8

>>> **Read an article from a book**

SPEAK AND READ

1 🔊 **Work in pairs. Look at the words in the box. Then answer the questions.**

| bus | café | coffee | hotel | music | radio | taxi | train |

1 What are the words in your language?
2 Which words are the same or very similar in your language? Circle them.

2 ▶1.16 **Read the beginning of the article. What's an international word?**

WORLDWIDE WORDS FOR KIDS

International words are the same or very similar in many different languages. With international words you can talk to people from different countries. When you go on vacation, do these things and use the international words in **bold**.

1 Take a **taxi** or **metro**. (*Bus* and *train* are similar in some languages, but they aren't international words.)

2 Find a **Wi-Fi** hotspot. Use the **internet** on your **telephone** to check **emails**, listen to the **radio**, or watch **music videos**.

3 Go to a **café** or a **bar**. Drink **tea** (with **lemon**) or **coffee**.

4 Go to a **restaurant**. Eat a **pizza** with a **salad**.

5 Visit a **museum**, go to a **park**, or go to a movie **theater**. Or stay in your **hotel** and watch **sports** on **television**!

3 **Read the rest of the article. Match sections 1–5 to the categories in the box.**

| Drinks | Food | Places | Technology | Transportation |

4 **Read the article again. Which words in Exercise 1 are international words?**

REACT

5 **Work in pairs. Choose your five favorite international words. Then compare with your partner.**

>>> Workbook, page 9

>>> Talk about one or more things

READ >>> **Grammar in context**

1 Read Stella's list of likes and dislikes. Which of your likes and dislikes are the same?

SOCIAL SCENE

LIKES 👍
- math classes (We have a great teacher.)
- the people in my drama group
- an ice-cream cone on a hot day
- old jeans
- the internet

DISLIKES 👎
- big cities (They're really noisy!)
- the school bus (It's always full.)
- video games (boring! 😒)
- sunglasses
- school lunches

STUDY

2 Complete the examples. Use Exercise 1 to help you.

Plural nouns

game > _games_

box > _____   class > _____
_____ > bu_ses_   lun_ch_ > _____
city > _____

Irregular plurals

man > men   woman > women
person > _____   foot > feet

See GRAMMAR DATABASE, page 98.

3 Complete the examples. Use Exercise 1 to help you.

Articles *a, an, the*

We have _____a_____ great math teacher.
Use *an* before *a, e, i, o, u.*
I like an _____ cone on a _____ day.
Use *the* for specific things.
The _____ is always full.
Don't use *the* for general things in the plural form.
I don't like ~~the~~ video _____.

See GRAMMAR DATABASE, page 98.

PRACTICE

4 Write the singular nouns.

singular	plural
1 _category_	categories
2 _____	videos
3 _____	sandwiches
4 _____	women

5 Write the things in the pictures.

apple   ~~day~~   glass   man   sandwich   story

1 _three days_   4 _____

2 _____   5 _____

3 _____   6 _____

6 Choose the correct options in the profile.

PROFILE

I'm from Washington, DC. It's (1) *a* / *(the)* capital city of the USA. It's (2) *a* / *the* very big city. I love (3) *the* / *–* cars, and I have (4) *a* / *the* big poster of an Italian sports car in my room. I like (5) *the* / *–* video games too. I have (6) *a* / *an* Xbox and (7) *a* / *an* PlayStation. My favorite sport is basketball. I play on (8) *a* / *the* school basketball team.

7 Complete the sentences with *a/an, the,* or –.

ALL ABOUT ME!

1 I like _____–_____ apples.
2 I don't like _____ color orange.
3 I take _____ taxi to school.
4 I love _____ internet.
5 I have _____ old phone.
6 I don't like _____ pizza.

WRITE AND SPEAK

8 a Write five sentences about you, three true and two false.

I'm …   I have …
My favorite …   I like / don't like …

b Work in pairs. Say your sentences. Your partner says "true" or "false."

>>> **Listen to a description of where things are from**

WORK WITH WORDS Countries and nationalities

1 a ▶1.17 **Work in pairs. Write the correct numbers in the table. Then listen and check.**

Number	Country	Nationality
	Brazil	Brazilian
	Germany	Germ........
	Italy	Ital........
	Japan	Japan........
	South Africa	South Africa........
	Turkey	Turk........

b ▶1.18 **Try to complete the nationalities. Add -an, -ese, -ian, -n, or -ish to the words. Listen and check. Then listen and repeat.**

2 Work in pairs. Think of something famous for each country. Then make a class list.

SPEAK AND LISTEN

3 a Work in pairs. Guess where Steve's things are from. Use countries from Exercise 1.

b ▶1.19 **Steve is talking about where his things are from. Listen and check your ideas.**

4 ▶1.19 **Listen again and choose the correct answer.**

1 Steve's from …
   Ⓐ the USA.   **B** Italy.   **C** Turkey.
2 Steve says, "It's a small world" because his things are all from …
   A the same part of the world.
   B different parts of the world.
   C very far away.
3 Where's Steve's friend Ricardo from?
   A Colombia   **B** Brazil   **C** the USA

REACT

5 🔊 **Work in pairs. Say where your things are from.**

LISTENING TIP

Before you listen, think: "What do I know about this topic?" Use your answer to help you understand.

PHRASE BYTES

My jeans / sunglasses are from …

Where's your T-shirt / bag from?

What's on the label?

It says … on the label.

I don't know.

MOVE BEYOND

Do the Words & Beyond exercise on page 106.

>>> **Talk about the things around you**

READ AND LISTEN >>> Grammar in context

1 ▶1.20 **Read and listen to the conversation. Write the names of the fruit.**

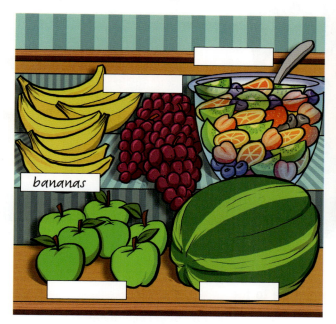

bananas

Zoe: We need to buy fruit.
Rose: OK. What about those bananas?
Zoe: I don't like bananas. But these apples are delicious.
Rose: They're very green. What's the name of those purple things?
Zoe: Those are grapes. They aren't my favorite fruit.
Rose: And what's this?
Zoe: It's a watermelon. But look at that fruit salad. That has a lot of different fruit in it.
Rose: OK. Let's buy fruit salad.

STUDY

2 **Complete the table with words from Exercise 1.**

This/that, these/those
Use *this* and *these* to talk about objects near you. Use *that* and *those* for objects far from you.

Here	There
Singular What's *this* ?	**Singular** Look at _____ fruit salad.
Plural _____ apples are delicious.	**Plural** *Those* are grapes.

See GRAMMAR DATABASE, page 98.

PRACTICE

3 **Complete the sentences with *this*, *that*, *these*, and *those*.**

1 I like *those* T-shirts.
2 _____ blue T-shirt's nice.
3 What about _____ sunglasses?
4 I don't like _____ bag.
5 _____ jeans are cool.
6 Do you like _____ soccer shirt?

4 **Complete the conversation with *this*, *that*, *these*, and *those*.**

Zoe: Wow! Look at these things.
Rose: Yes! I love (1) *those* . Great postcards!
Zoe: And (2) _____ 's a really old tennis racket!
Rose: What's (3) _____ in English?
Zoe: It's a bowl.
Rose: It's nice. And what are (4) _____ ?
Zoe: They're sports cards. And (5) _____ is an album for the cards.

SPEAK

5 **Work in pairs. Put your things on your desk. Ask and answer questions about them.**

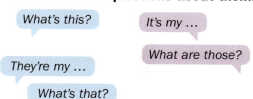

What's this?

It's my …

What are those?

They're my …

What's that?

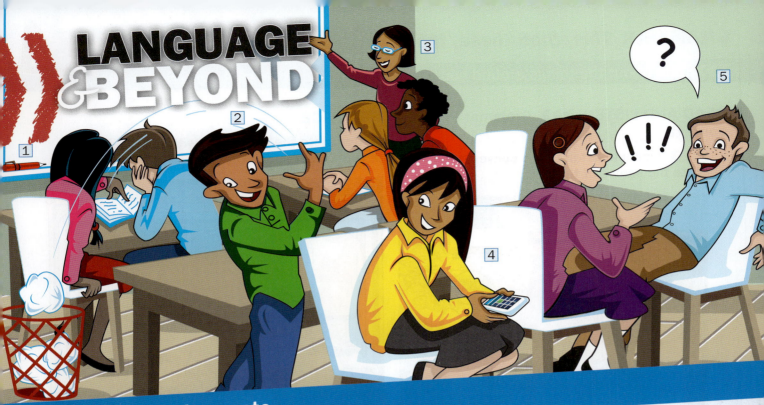

LANGUAGE &BEYOND

>>> Be a good classmate

SPEAK AND READ

1 a Work in pairs. Match the situations (1–5) in the picture to the descriptions (a–e).

b Do you do these things in class? Write *never* (0%), *sometimes* (50%), or *always* (100%). Then compare your answers with the rest of your class.

a be noisy _____
b help classmates _____
c be quiet and listen to the teacher _____
d throw trash in the wastebasket _____
e use a phone _____

DO

2 a Work in pairs. Write the things in Exercise 1a in the correct column. Can you add more things?

It's good to … in class.	It's bad to … in class.

b Why are the things good or bad? Complete the sentences with a word or phrase from Exercise 1.

1 If you're _____ , you can hear the teacher.
2 If you're _____ , you can't hear other students.
3 If you _____ , they can understand the lesson too.
4 If you _____ , the classroom is clean.

REFLECT

3  Talk about the questions. Then read the **REFLECTION POINT**.

1 Are you a good classmate?
2 Why is it important to be a good classmate?
3 What can you change in your class?

EXTEND

4 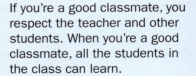 Work in groups. Write two good things and two bad things for one of these situations.

It's good/bad to … at home.
It's good/bad to … with my friends.

PHRASE BYTES

I'm / I'm not …

It's important because …

We need to … more.

REFLECTION POINT

If you're a good classmate, you respect the teacher and other students. When you're a good classmate, all the students in the class can learn.

SCHOOL SKILLS

16

>>> Describe things

SPEAK

1 Work in pairs. Match the adjectives to their opposites.

1	big	a	new (for things)
2	old	b	horrible
3	quiet	c	small
4	nice	d	noisy

LISTEN

2 ▶1.21 **Listen to the conversations. What things do the people describe?**

1
Becca: I can't find my (1) _____ .
Kent: What color is it?
Becca: It's red, and it's really (2) _____ .
Kent: Is that it on the chair?
Becca: Yes, that's it.

2
Anita: Do you like Vicky's (3) _____ ? They're (4) _____ .
Zac: They're very (5) _____ .
Vicky: Thanks. They're (6) _____ .

3
Zac: What's your house like?
Lily: It's OK, but the neighbors are really (7) _____ .
Zac: What about your (8) _____ ? Is it (9) _____ ?
Lily: No, my room's very (10) _____ .

3 ▶1.21 **Complete the conversations. Then listen again and check.**

4 ▶1.22 **Listen and repeat the sentences from the conversations.**

ACT

5 🗇 **Work in pairs. Complete the tasks.**

- Choose a conversation from Exercise 2.
- Write a similar conversation about a different thing.
- Practice the conversation.
- Present the conversation to other students. Don't read it.

PHRASEBOOK ▶1.23

Ask for a description of something

What color is it?

What's / What are your … like?

Is it big / small?

Describe something

It's black / red.

They're Italian / Brazilian.

They're very / really nice.

The neighbors are noisy / quiet.

>>> Workbook, page 15

WRITING My things

>>> Write a description of a thing

SPEAK AND READ

1 a Work in pairs. Look at the pictures and describe them. Note the adjectives (*big*, *blue*) you use.

b Read the descriptions. Do they use the same adjectives?

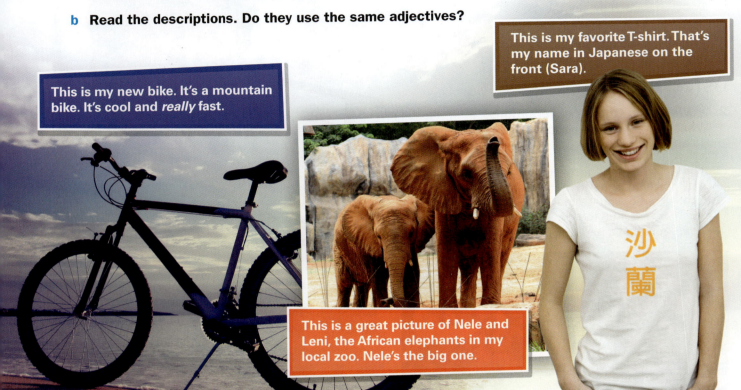

This is my favorite T-shirt. That's my name in Japanese on the front (Sara).

This is my new bike. It's a mountain bike. It's cool and *really* fast.

This is a great picture of Nele and Leni, the African elephants in my local zoo. Nele's the big one.

2 Read the tips in the **HOW TO** box. Then <u>underline</u> other adjectives in the picture descriptions.

HOW TO ⦰

write a description of a thing

- ■ Use *am* / *are* / *is* + adjective: *it's cool*.
- ■ Use adjective + noun: *my **favorite T-shirt***.
- ■ Use *really* / *very* + adjective: ***really fast***.

PRACTICE

3 Put the words in order to make sentences.

1 phone. / my / is / This / new

2 nice / are / sunglasses. / really / These

3 of Japanese / This / collection / my / comics. / is

4 very / My / fast. / isn't / computer

5 really / jeans / are / favorite / old. / My

DISCUSS

4 Talk about one thing you have at school. What color is it? Is it old or new? Do you like it? Is it your favorite?

WRITE

5 Write a description of three things.

1 Choose three things. Use photos or draw pictures of the three things.
2 Use adjectives to describe each thing. What color is it? Is it big or small? Is it old or new?
3 Remember that adjectives come before the noun. Start sentences about your thing with "It." See the **HOW TO** box.

SHARE

6 Take turns reading your descriptions. Listen to your classmates. Name one picture and description you like.

>>>> Workbook, pages 16–17

VOCABULARY Things

1 Complete the things.

YourThings — THE WEBSITE FOR YOU AND YOUR THINGS

• HOME • PROFILE
• ABOUT • SEARCH
YOUR THINGS

1 s _____

2 T-s _____

3 i _____ c _____

4 s _____
b _____

5 b _____ p _____

6 b _____

7 p _____

8 g _____
c _____ e _____

___ /8

Countries and nationalities

2 Complete the countries and nationalities.

1 Juliana's my Braz_____ pen pal. She's from Rio de Janeiro in Braz_____ .

2 These jeans are from Ital_____ . I love Ital_____ fashion.

3 My dad's South Afric_____ , and South Afric_____ is my favorite soccer team.

4 I want to go to Turk_____ . I love Turk_____ food!

5 I'm Yoshi, and I'm Jap_____ . I'm from Osaka, in the south of Jap_____ .

6 Are you from Germ_____ ? I want to practice my Germ_____ .

___ /12

GRAMMAR Plural nouns; *a/an, the*

3 Complete the message with *a*, *an*, *the*, *–*, or the plural of the noun in parentheses.

My name's Vasily, and I live in (1) _____ city in Russia called Gatchina. It isn't one of Russia's famous (2) _____ (city), but it's (3) _____ interesting place. I love technology and (4) _____ computers. (5) _____ science teachers at my school are great, and I learn a lot in their (6) _____ (class). I love (7) _____ internet too. I have (8) _____ website with a lot of my (9) _____ (video) on it.

___ /18

This/that, these/those

4 Complete the description with *this*, *that*, *these*, and *those*.

YourThings

Hi, everyone! (1) _____ is my room. All my favorite things are in here. (2) _____ are my favorite jeans. I love them! (3) _____ phone isn't very new, but I still use it. (4) _____ sunglasses are from my local market. They're really cool. (5) _____ 's my game console. And you see (6) _____ soccer ball? It has Neymar's signature on it. ☺

___ /12

Your score: ___ /50

SKILLS CHECK

✓✓✓	Yes, I can. No problem!
✓✓	Yes, I can. But I need a little help.
✓	Yes, I can. But I need a lot of help.

I can read an article from a book. _____
I can listen to a description of where things are from. _____
I can be a good classmate. _____
I can describe things. _____
I can write a description of a thing. _____

PEOPLE

IN THE PICTURE Family and friends

>>> Talk about your family and friends

WORK WITH WORDS Family

1 **RECALL** Work in pairs. Write the opposites. You have one minute.

1 same – _____
2 nice – _____
3 _____ – small
4 bad – _____
5 _____ – quiet
6 old – _____ (for things), young (for people)

2 a Work in pairs. Look at the pictures on 12-year-old Leo's phone. Which are friends? Which are family members?

> **PHRASE BYTES**
>
> I think the boy / girl in picture 1 … is a friend / family member.
>
> I think the man / woman in picture … is …

b ▶1.24 Listen and check your answers. Match the names to the correct pictures.

Carlos _____ Dan _____ Emma _____

3 a ▶1.24 Listen again. Match the family words to the pictures.

brother _____ dad _____ father _____ grandchild _____
grandfather _____ grandma _____ grandmother _____ grandpa _____
mom _____ mother _____ only child _____ sister _____

b ▶1.25 Listen and check.

4 a ▶1.26 **PRONOUNCE** Listen and repeat the /æ/ sound in these words.

Dad   bad   banana

b ▶1.27 Listen and repeat these words.

am   black   café   grandma   grandpa   Japan   Saturday
that

5 Work in pairs. Ask and answer.

> Who's in picture 3?

> That's Leo's grandma and grandpa.

6 **THE MOVING PICTURE** ▶ Watch the video about Leo's friend, Dan. Who does Dan meet? Are they family or friends?

PEOPLE

PHONE

PEOPLE

MESSAGES

SETTINGS

SPEAK

7 Work in pairs. Draw a picture of your family or show pictures. Talk about your family.

PHRASE BYTES

This is my dad / sister.

He's / She's ... years old.

He's / She's from Chile.

He's / She's quiet / noisy / great / horrible / very nice.

MOVE BEYOND

Do the Words & Beyond exercise on page 107.

>>> **Read text messages**

SPEAK AND READ

1 🗣 Work in pairs. Write eight names for your phone contact list. Then tell your partner about your list.

2 ▶1.28 Look at the pictures and read the first sentence of each message. Who are the messages from? Who are they for?

READING TIP ✓

Look at the type of text. It can help you understand what it's about.

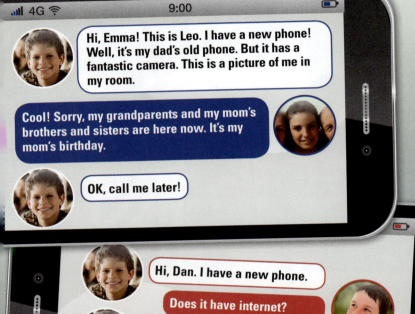

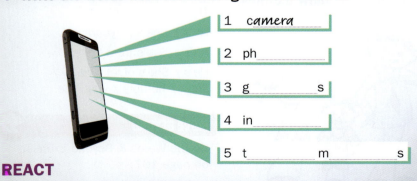

3 Read the messages and write the name(s).

1 _____ are game players.
2 _____ has the wrong number.
3 _____ is in his room.
4 _____ is at a birthday party.
5 _____ have a lot of homework.
6 _____ isn't happy about text messages in class.

4 Write the words from the messages in Exercise 2.

1 camera
2 ph_____
3 g_____ s_____
4 in_____
5 t_____ m_____ s_____

PHRASE BYTES

In my school it's OK / it isn't OK to use phones in …
I use my phone for calls / pictures.

REACT

5 🗣 Work in pairs. Ask and answer the questions.

1 Is it OK to use phones at your school? When and where?
2 What do you or your friends use your phones for?

MOVE BEYOND

Write a message from Leo to a different person from pages 20–21. Write one or two sentences.

>>> Workbook, page 21

READ AND LISTEN >>> Grammar in context

1 ▶1.29 **Read and listen to the conversation. Complete the sentences.**

It's Clara's dad's _____ on Saturday. Clara doesn't have a _____ .

Clara: I have a problem.
Albert: What?
Clara: I don't have a present for my dad's birthday on Saturday.
Albert: Does he have a pen for his tablet? That's a good present.
Clara: No, he doesn't. He doesn't have a tablet. He has a laptop.
Albert: OK. Do you have an idea?
Clara: No, I don't. And I don't have much time for shopping.
Albert: Oh. You're right. You have a problem.

STUDY

2 **Complete the examples. Use Exercise 1 to help you.**

Have (*I, you, we, they*)

Affirmative – *have*	Negative – *don't have*
I _have_ a problem.	I _____ a present.

Questions	Short answers
_Do_ you have a problem?	Yes, I do.
_____ you have an idea?	No, I _____ .

Has (*he, she, it*)

Affirmative – *has*	Negative – *doesn't have*
Clara _has_ a problem.	She _doesn't have_ a present.
He _____ a laptop.	He _____ a tablet.

Questions	Short answers
Does he have a laptop?	Yes, he _____ .
_____ he have a tablet?	No, he _doesn't_ .

See GRAMMAR DATABASE, page 99.

PRACTICE

3 **Complete Clara's sentences with *have* or *don't have*.**

I (1) _____*have*_____ a great room! It's very big, but I (2) _____ a TV. We (3) _____ one television in our house, but it isn't in my room! I (4) _____ a computer. It's old. My brothers (5) _____ an Xbox. It's new, and they (6) _____ a lot of games – only four or five.

4 **Write about Albert. What does he have? What doesn't he have?**

He has three sisters.

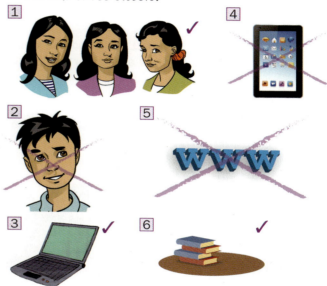

5 ▶1.30 **Complete the conversation. Then listen and check.**

Clara: (1) ____*Do*____ you have a favorite movie?
Lila: No, I (2) _____ . What about you?
Clara: Yes, I (3) _____ . It's *School Days*.
Lila: (4) _____ it have Kristin Stone in it?
Clara: No, it (5) _____ . It's with Mila King.
Lila: Oh yes. (6) _____ you have it?
Clara: Yes, I (7) _____ . We can watch it together.

6 **Write three more questions for a partner.**

Survey

- Do you have a TV in your room?
- Do you have a big family?
- Do you have a favorite movie?

SPEAK

7 **Work in pairs. Ask and answer the questions you both wrote in Exercise 6.**

>>> Listen to a quiz show

WORK WITH WORDS Parts of the body

1 🔊 **Look at Mandy's pictures of parts of the body. What do you think?**

2 a ▶1.31 **Listen and point to the correct parts of the body in the pictures.**

  b ▶1.32 **Listen and repeat the parts of the body.**

arm	back	ear	eye	face	foot	hand
head	leg	mouth	nose	teeth		

3 a **Work in pairs. Student A: look at page 115. Read the description to your partner. Student B: draw and color the picture.**

  b **Student B: look at page 116. Read the description to your partner. Student A: draw and color the picture.**

PHRASE BYTES

I think they're good / original.

I like / don't like them.

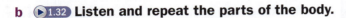

SPEAK AND LISTEN

4 **Work in pairs. Look at the pictures and choose the correct answer.**

FAMOUS
>> PARTS OF THE BODY
QUIZ 👁

1 Whose mouth is this?
A Beyoncé's
B the Mona Lisa's
C Shakira's

2 Whose hands are these?
A Batman's
B Mario's
C Mickey Mouse's

3 Whose legs are these?
A Mario Balotelli's
B Neymar's
C Lionel Messi's

4 Whose ear is this?
A Frodo Baggins's (*The Hobbit*)
B Mr. Spock's (*Star Trek*)
C Daniel Craig's (*James Bond*)

5  Whose eye is this?
A Jennifer Lawrence's
B Cleopatra's
C Lady Gaga's

5 ▶1.33 **Listen to the quiz. Check your answers. Who's the winner – Kim or Alan?**

6 ▶1.33 **Listen again. What's special about the things in the five pictures?**

1 *Her smile is special.*   2 *His hands are …*

PHRASE BYTES

I think / don't think it's a good game.

I have blue eyes / nice feet.

I have big feet. My dad has big feet too.

I have long legs like my mom.

REACT

7 🔊 **Work in pairs. Ask and answer the questions.**

1 Is this a good quiz game?
2 Do you have the same eyes or legs as people in your family?

MOVE BEYOND

Do the Words & Beyond exercise on page 107.

>>>> Workbook, pages 24–25

>>> **Talk about your things, family, and friends**

READ AND LISTEN >>> Grammar in context

1 ▶1.34 **Read and listen to the conversation. Which legs in the picture are Amy's legs?**

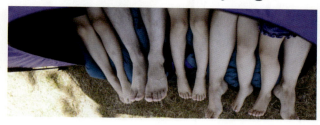

Amy: Hi, Nick! This is a picture from our camping trip!
Nick: Cool! Whose legs are they?
Amy: My mom's, my dad's, my sister's, her friend's, and mine. My two brothers' legs aren't in the picture.
Nick: Which legs are yours?
Amy: My sister's friend Ellen is in the middle. On the right are my mom's and my sister's legs. Theirs are together. Dad is on the other side of Ellen. Those legs with the big feet are his. And mine are the nice legs!

STUDY

2 **Complete the examples. Use Exercise 1 to help you.**

Possessive *'s/s'* and *Whose?*
Noun + *'s*   My sister has two legs. → My _sister's_ legs …
Regular plural noun + *s'*   My brothers have two legs. → My _____ legs …
***Whose* + noun**   _____ legs are they?

3 **Complete the table with possessive pronouns. Use Exercise 1 to help you.**

Possessive adjectives and possessive pronouns	
My legs are the nice legs.	_Mine_ *are the nice legs.*
Which are your legs?	*Which legs are* _____ ?
Those big feet are my dad's feet.	*Those big feet are* _____.
These big feet are my mom's feet.	*These big feet are hers.*
All of these legs are our legs.	*All of these legs are ours.*
Their legs are together.	_____ *are together.*

See **GRAMMAR DATABASE**, page 99.

PRACTICE

4 **Complete Amy's sentences with *'s* or *s'* and a part of the body.**

1 That's _my sister's tooth_ (my sister).

4 Those are _____ (my grandpa).

2 Those are _____ (my brothers).

5 Those are _____ (my friends).

3 Those are _____ (my grandparents).

6 That's _____ (my mom).

5 **Complete the answers with the correct possessive pronouns.**

Teacher: Whose homework is this?
Student: I think it's Lucy's homework. Yes, it's (1) _hers_ .
Teacher: Whose pen is this?
Student: I think it's my pen. Yes, it's (2) _____ .
Teacher: Whose bags are these?
Student: I think they're Diego's and Felipe's. Yes, they're (3) _____ .
Teacher: Whose tablet is this?
Student: I think it's Mr. Cole's. Yes, it's (4) _____ .
Teacher: Whose books are these?
Student: I think they're our books. Yes, they're (5) _____ .
Teacher: Whose glasses are these?
Student: I think they're your glasses. Yes, they're (6) _____ , Ms. Carter!

SPEAK

6 **Play *Whose chair is it?***

■ Walk around the room. When your teacher says "Stop," sit down. Say whose chair you're in.

I'm in Valentina's chair.   *Yes, that's hers.*

That isn't hers. That's Ana's chair.

LANGUAGE &BEYOND

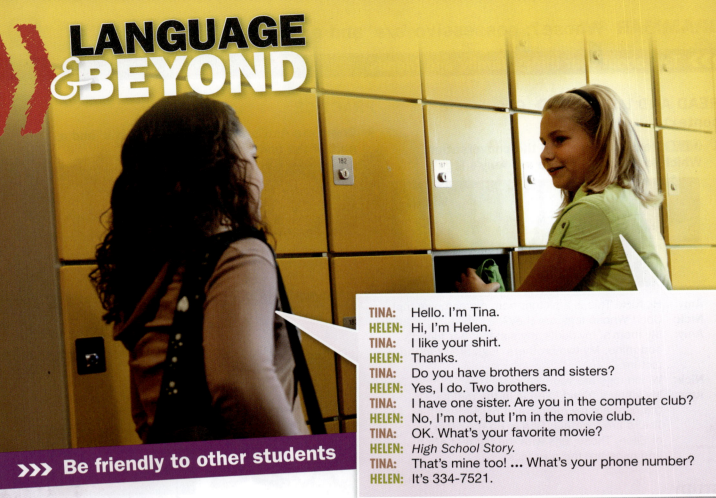

TINA: Hello. I'm Tina.
HELEN: Hi, I'm Helen.
TINA: I like your shirt.
HELEN: Thanks.
TINA: Do you have brothers and sisters?
HELEN: Yes, I do. Two brothers.
TINA: I have one sister. Are you in the computer club?
HELEN: No, I'm not, but I'm in the movie club.
TINA: OK. What's your favorite movie?
HELEN: *High School Story.*
TINA: That's mine too! ... What's your phone number?
HELEN: It's 334-7521.

SCHOOL SKILLS

>>> Be friendly to other students

READ

1 ▶1.35 **Read and listen to the conversation. What do the girls have in common?**

DO

2 **Number the "Make friends" tips in the correct order. Use Exercise 1 to help you.**

3 **Match the sentences to tips a–e in Exercise 2. There's an extra sentence.**

1 Your shoes are nice. _____
2 Do you have a brother? _____
3 What's your address? _____
4 Hello. _____
5 Who's your favorite soccer player? _____
6 Are you on the soccer team? _____

REFLECT

4 **Talk about the questions. Then read the** **REFLECTION POINT** .

1 Do you have a lot of friends? Or do you have one or two good friends?
2 Where are your friends from (school, clubs, teams, your street)?
3 Is it easy or hard for you to make new friends?

EXTEND

5 a **Write questions to ask about your family and favorite things: movies, TV programs, stars, and sports teams.**

b **Make new friends in class. Walk around and ask other students your questions.**

MAKE FRIENDS – IT'S EASY!

_____ a Ask for an address or phone number.
_____ b Ask questions about favorite movies or stars, or clubs and teams.
_____ c Say something nice.
_____ d Smile ☺ and say hello.
_____ e Ask questions about family.

PHRASE BYTES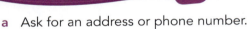

I have …

My friends are from school.

It's easy for me to make new friends. I like to talk to people.

It's hard for me. I'm quiet.

REFLECTION POINT

It isn't important to have a lot of friends. But new friends are interesting. Talk to people and make new friends!

SPEAK

1 **How many phones does your family have? Do you have a cell phone? Does your family have a phone in your house?**

LISTEN

2 ▶ 1.36 **Listen to the conversations. What happens in each phone call?**

A The person has the wrong number.
B The person has a new number.
C The person spells a long name.

1

Felix:	Hello?
Mrs. Zemontas:	Hi, Felix. This is Mrs. Zemontas. Can I speak to your (1) _____ ?
Felix:	She isn't here right now.
Mrs. Zemontas:	OK, (2) _____ she call me, please? It's Emily Zemontas.
Felix:	Um … Can you spell (3) _____ , please?
Mrs. Zemontas:	Z-E-M-O-N-T-A-S.
Felix:	OK, Mrs. Zemontas.
Mrs. Zemontas:	Thanks, Felix. Bye.

2

Felix:	Hel- …
Kelly:	Hi, are you at the movies?
Felix:	(4) _____ , I don't understand. What movie?
Kelly:	Is this Josh?
Felix:	No, it isn't. You have the wrong (5) _____ .
Kelly:	Oh, I'm sorry. Bye.

3

Felix:	Hello?
Mark:	Hi, Felix, this is Mark. Is Kyle there?
Felix:	No, he isn't.
Mark:	Can you give him my new cell phone number?
Felix:	Sure.
Mark:	It's 830-0315.
Felix:	830 … Sorry, can (6) _____ repeat that?
Mark:	830-0315.
Felix:	830-0315. OK.
Mark:	Thanks. Bye.

---

3 **a** ▶ 1.36 **Listen again and complete the conversations.**

  b ▶ 1.37 **Listen to the sentences and check. Then listen and repeat.**

4 **Work in pairs. Read and practice the conversations in Exercise 2.**

ACT

5 🗎 **Work in pairs. Read the situations below. Act out the conversations.**

  1 Student A: call Student B.
    A: Ask for Student B's father. Your name is Jo Honeycomb.
    B: Your father isn't at home. Ask the person to spell his/her name.

  2 Student B: call Student A.
    B: Ask if Student A is at the museum. Ask if it's Ben.
    A: You don't understand. It's a wrong number.

  3 Student A: call Student B.
    A: Ask for Sam. Your name's Charlie, and your phone number is 765-5421.
    B: Sam isn't at home. Ask Student A to repeat his/her number.

PHRASEBOOK ▶ 1.38

Make a call

Can I speak to … ?

Is this … ?

Is … there?

Can he / she call me, please?

Answer a call

Can you spell that, please?

Sorry, can you repeat that?

Sorry, I don't understand.

You have the wrong number.

Bye. / Goodbye.

WRITING My favorite person

>>> Write a description of a person

READ

1 Describe the people in the pictures. You can use words from the box.

> friendly   funny   gray hair   happy   nice   old   small   smart

2 Read Kim's description of her grandmother. Match it to the correct picture. <u>Underline</u> the important words.

Write about your favorite senior.
My Grandma, by Sophie

My grandma, Daisy, is my dad's mother. She's about 65. She's very smart and friendly. She has black and gray hair, very small feet, and a small nose. Grandma has four grandchildren, but I'm the only girl. Her house is very nice, and it has a big yard. It's near our house in Chicago.

3 Read the tips in the **HOW TO** box. Then circle the apostrophes in the description in Exercise 2. Are they for missing letters or possessives?

HOW TO ❓

use apostrophes (')

- Use for a missing letter (*you are = you're*).
- Use with possessive *'s* or *s'* (*my brother's eyes, my two sisters' eyes*).

PRACTICE

4 Read the description. Put in apostrophes.

> My brothers 14. He has very big feet. My brothers room has a lot of clothes and things everywhere. My two sisters rooms arent like that.

DISCUSS

5 Talk about an important person in your life. Is this person a friend or family? Describe the person's face. Talk about the person's family.

WRITE

6 Describe an important person in your life.

> **1** Say who the important person is. Describe the person's hair and eyes. Describe his or her family and favorite things.
> **2** Use "has" or "doesn't have" to write about the person's family or things.
> **3** Use apostrophe s ('s) to write about things or features the person has. See the **HOW TO** box.

SHARE

7 Take turns reading your descriptions. Listen to your classmates. Which person do you want to meet? Name one interesting thing you remember about each person.

>>> Workbook, pages 28–29

VOCABULARY Family

1 Complete the picture description.

SUPERSTAR HAKAN AT HOME

This is my family. Here's my
(1) m_____ and
(2) f_____ . My (3) m_____ and
(4) d_____ are my number one fans. This is my
(5) g_____ m
and my (6) g_____ f_____ .
I call them (7) G_____ and
(8) G_____ . I'm their only
(9) g_____ . I'm an
(10) o_____ c_____ , so I don't
have (11) b_____ s or
(12) s_____ s.   ___ /12

Parts of the body

2 Write the parts of the body from the box.

arm	back	ear	eye	face	foot
hand	head	leg	mouth	nose	teeth

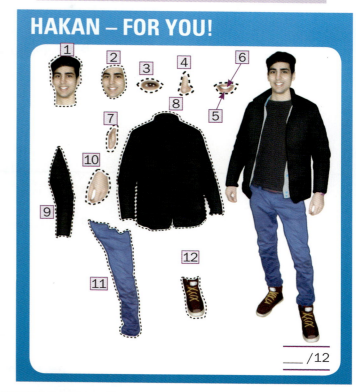

HAKAN – FOR YOU!

___ /12

GRAMMAR *Have*

3 Complete the interview with the correct form of *have* and *do*, *does*, or *don't*.

Kate: You (1) _____ a cool house.
(2) _____ it _____
a lot of rooms?
Hakan: Yes, it (3) _____ . It
(4) _____ 10 rooms for my
family and me. All the rooms
(5) _____ TVs and music
players.
Kate: (6) _____ you
a special singing room?
Hakan: No, I (7) _____ . I sing in all
the rooms!   ___ /14

Whose?; possessive *'s/s'* and possessive pronouns

4 Choose the correct options to complete the conversation.

Kate: (1) *Who's / Whose* room is this?
Hakan: This is my (2) *mom's / moms'* room.
Those sunglasses are (3) *hers / his* .
And this room is (4) *mine / yours* .
I have a lot of friends. Those are all my
(5) *friend's / friends'* things.
These clothes are (6) *ours / theirs* too.

___ /12

Your score: ___ /50

SKILLS CHECK

✓✓✓	Yes, I can. No problem!
✓✓	Yes, I can. But I need a little help.
✓	Yes, I can. But I need a lot of help.

I can read text messages. _____
I can listen to a quiz show. _____
I can be friendly to other students. _____
I can talk on the phone. _____
I can write a description of a person. _____

⟫⟫⟫ Workbook, pages 30–31

READ

1 Complete the five conversations. For each question, choose A, B, or C.

Example:

0 *Whose book is this?*

A *It's her.*

B *They're Lucy's.*

C *It's mine.*

TEST-TAKING TIPS

❓ answer multiple-choice questions

- Look at the example.
- Read each question. Read the answer choices (A–C).
- Decide which choices are definitely wrong. Look at meaning and grammar to help you.
- Read the question again. Check your answer.

1 *Do you have a brother?*

A *Yes, I do.*

B *No, I have a brother.*

C *Yes, one sister.*

2 *Are these your pictures?*

A *No, it isn't.*

B *No, they aren't.*

C *Yes, they're yours.*

3 *That's a nice bag.*

A *I can't find it.*

B *It has internet.*

C *Thanks. It's new.*

4 *Can you spell your name, please?*

A *P-L-E-A-S-E.*

B *It's P-E-R-E-Z.*

C *Yes, it's Felipe Perez.*

5 *You have the wrong number.*

A *Sorry, I don't know.*

B *Oh, I'm sorry.*

C *Sorry, she isn't here.*

Reading: _____ /10

LISTEN

2 **1.39** **Listen to a phone call about a drama group. Complete Ivy's notes.**

Drama group

Day:	(0)	_Saturday morning_
Number of people in group:	(1)	
Age of people in group:	(2)	years old
Place:	(3) Victoria	
Name of teacher:	(4) Ms.	
Teacher's phone number:	(5)	

Listening: _____ /10

TEST-TAKING TIPS

❓ listen and complete notes

- Look at the example. It shows you what to do.
- Read the other notes before you listen.
- Decide what type of information you need (names, numbers, …).
- Listen for this information. Write the numbers or words.
- When you listen again, check your answers.

WRITE

3 **Read the descriptions and complete the words for parts of the body.**

Example:

0	You hear with them.	e _a_ _r_ _s_
1	You look with them.	e _____
2	They're on your arms.	h _____
3	They're in your mouth.	t _____
4	You stand on them.	f _____
5	Your nose is on it.	f _____

_____ /5

TEST-TAKING TIPS

❓ complete words from descriptions

- Look at the example. Then look at each question.
- Read the description and the first letter. Can you think of the word?
- Check the number of letters. (One line is one letter.)
- Check your spelling.

4 **Read the message from your new friend Jason. Write a reply. Tell Jason about your family (25–35 words).**

> Tell me about your family. Do you have a big or a small family? Do you have any brothers or sisters? How old are the people in your family? Tell me about them.

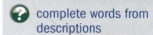 Reply

_____ /5

Writing: _____ / 10

Progress check score _____ /30

TEST-TAKING TIPS

❓ reply to an email or message

- Read the email or message.
- Write your reply. Answer all the questions in the email or message.
- Use the correct number of words.

3 ANIMAL MAGIC

IN THE PICTURE Adopt a pet

>>> Talk about pets

WORK WITH WORDS Pet animals

1 **RECALL** Work in pairs. Look at the pictures and write eight parts of the animals' bodies. You have one minute.

ear ...

2 a Match the pictures (a–j) to the words in the box.

bird _____	cat _____	chicken _____	dog _____	fish _____	hamster _____
horse _____	mouse _____	rabbit _____	turtle _____	

b ▶1.40 Listen and check your answers. Then listen and repeat.

3 a Read the messages and write animals from Exercise 2a.

b ▶1.41 Listen and check your answers.

4 a ▶1.42 Listen to five people talking about their pets. Write the animals from Exercise 2a.

1 Julia   *rabbit*
2 Brian   _____
3 Karen   _____
4 Leo   _____
5 Nicky   _____

b ▶1.42 Listen again and answer the questions.

1 Whose pet is named Minnie?
   Leo's pet is named Minnie.
2 Whose pet has big ears?
   _____
3 Whose pet has small eyes?
   _____
4 Whose pet doesn't have a name?
   _____

5 a ▶1.43 **PRONOUNCE** Listen and repeat the /ɪ/ sound in these words.

ch**i**cken   f**i**sh   rabb**i**t

b ▶1.44 Listen and repeat these words.

b**i**g   s**i**x   g**i**ve   c**i**ty   s**i**t

adopt a PET

🐾 HOME   🐾 ABOUT US   🐾 PETS

1 I'm from the United States. I'm five years old. I'm tall and black, and my name's Hank. I'm a good pet, and I'm also a good form of transportation.

2 I'm Lisa. Please adopt me! I'm one of the USA's favorite pets. I have two big brown eyes, four legs, and a big nose. I'm yellow.

3 My name's Sandra. I'm six months old. I'm a perfect pet because I give you food. Adopt me and eat eggs every day.

4 My name's Jimmy, and this is my brother, Jock. I'm black and white. Jock is yellow and black. We're one year old.

5 I'm Polly. I'm eight months old. I'm very friendly. I'm green, yellow, and black. Listen to me sing.

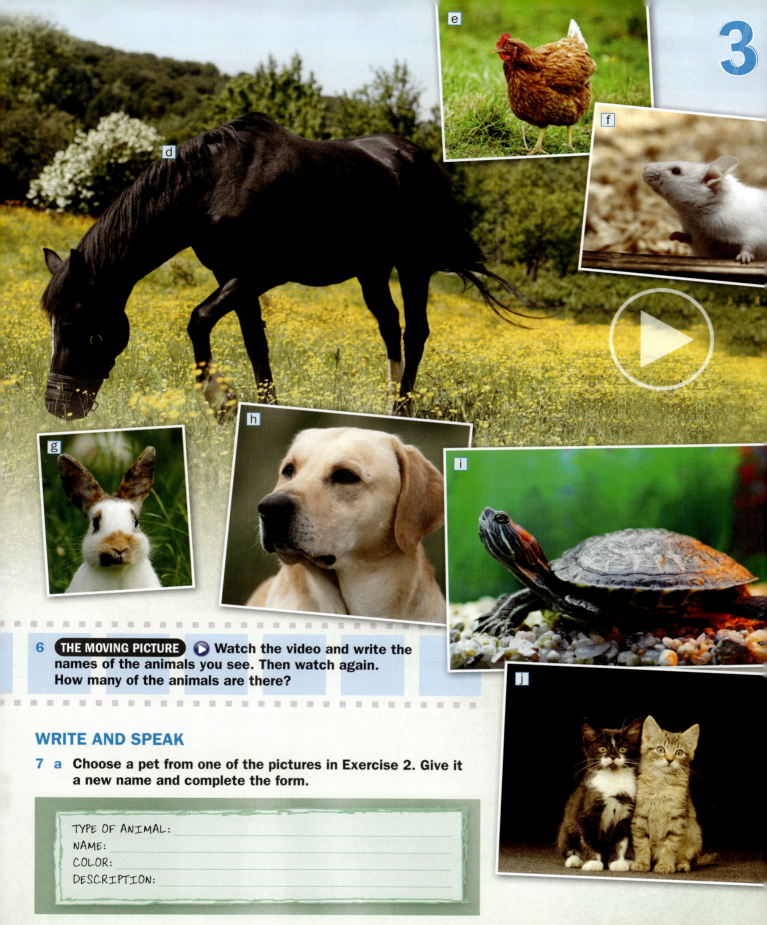

6 **THE MOVING PICTURE** ▶ **Watch the video and write the names of the animals you see. Then watch again. How many of the animals are there?**

WRITE AND SPEAK

7 a Choose a pet from one of the pictures in Exercise 2. Give it a new name and complete the form.

> TYPE OF ANIMAL: _____
> NAME: _____
> COLOR: _____
> DESCRIPTION: _____

b Work in pairs. Tell your partner about your new pet.

> My pet's a/an …
> Its name's …
>   It's …
>   It has …

MOVE BEYOND
Do the Words & Beyond exercise on page 108.

>>> **Read instructions**

SPEAK AND READ

1 🔊 **Work in pairs. Ask and answer the questions.**

1 What pets do you or your friends have?
2 What are their names?

2 ▶1.45 **Read the web page. What three things are important to remember?**

TEACH YOUR PET ENGLISH!

● HOME ● ABOUT US ● JOKES ● CONTACT US

> Hi. My name's Harry. How do you do? I can speak English!

Do you have a pet dog, bird, or rabbit? Do you talk to your pet in Spanish, Turkish, or Russian? Now you can teach your pet English. Use these simple orders and instructions. Don't forget – they aren't for all kinds of pets.

Here (Come here.)

Sit (Sit down.)
Stay / Wait (Don't move.)

Down (Lie down.)
Up (Stand up.)

Quiet (Be quiet!)
No (Don't do that!)

Here are some more unusual instructions …

Shake (Shake hands.)

Fetch (Find something and come back.)

Remember: Always be nice to your pet. Say …
Good boy! / Good girl!

Finally, here are some more things to say to your pet in English:
Hello / Good morning / Good night (+ name of pet)
Walk time! (It's time for a walk.)
Food! (It's time to eat.)

It's important to say the orders in the right way.

CLICK HERE TO LISTEN AND PRACTICE THE ORDERS.

3 Work in pairs.
Student A: mime an instruction from the web page.
Student B: say the instruction without looking at the page. Then change roles.

REACT

4 🔊 **Work in pairs. Ask and answer the questions.**

1 Are pets popular in your country? Which ones?
2 Do you talk to animals? In which language?
3 Do animals understand you?

READ AND LISTEN >>> Grammar in context

1 a Read the conversation. What pet does Laura have – a horse, a chicken, or a hamster?

Mom: Happy birthday, Laura!
Dad: Don't look! OK. Open your eyes.
Laura: Wow, is that for me? A pet _____ !
Mom: It's for you. Find a quiet place for it.
Laura: Is it a boy or a girl?
Mom: It's a boy.
Dad: Don't put him in your room. They play at night.
Mom: Dad has a book for us.
Dad: Yes. It says, "Give them some food and water every day." Don't forget.
Laura: Yes, Dad. Thanks!
Dad: It's all Mom's idea. Thank her!

b ▶1.46 **Listen and check your answer.**

STUDY

2 Complete the examples. Use Exercise 1 to help you.

Imperatives	
Affirmative	**Negative**
Open your eyes.	_Don't_ look!
_____ a	_____ him in
quiet place for it.	your room.

See GRAMMAR DATABASE, page 100.

3 Complete the table. Use Exercise 1 to help you.

Object pronouns	
Subject pronouns	**Object pronouns**
_It's_ a boy.	_Find a quiet place for_ _it_ .
I	Is that for _____ ?
you	It's for _____ .
he	Don't put _____ in your room.
she	Thank _____ !
it	Find a quiet place for _____ .
we	Dad has a book for _____ .
they	Give _____ some food and water every day.

See GRAMMAR DATABASE, page 100.

PRACTICE

4 Choose the correct options to complete the sentences.

TIPS ABOUT HAMSTERS

1 _Keep_ / _Don't keep_ your hamster in a hot place.
2 _Be_ / _Don't be_ nice to it.
3 _Give_ / _Don't give_ it water and food every day.
4 _Say_ / _Don't say_ bad things to your hamster.
5 _Play_ / _Don't play_ with it.
6 _Take_ / _Don't take_ your hamster to your English class.

5 Match the sentences (1–5) to the pictures (a–e).

1 Don't walk on the grass. _c_
2 Close the door. _____
3 Please be quiet. _____
4 Don't cross the street. _____
5 Don't play ball games. _____

6 Complete Laura's teacher's instructions. Use object pronouns.

1 "Class, I'm your teacher and I'm talking. Look at _me_ (your teacher)."
2 "Jack, go to the door and open _____ (the door)."
3 "Helen, find some pens and give _____ (the pens) to Roberto."
4 "Lucas doesn't have his book. Sandra, help _____ (Lucas)."
5 "It's Laura's birthday. Let's say 'Happy birthday' to _____ (Laura)."
6 "Laura, we have something for you. Here's a small present from _____ (me and your classmates)."

SPEAK

7 Work in pairs. Take turns. Give and follow instructions.

Go to the door.

Give me your pen.

Don't talk.

WORK WITH WORDS Things in your room

1 Work in pairs. Look at the pictures and answer the questions.

1 What animals can you see in the pictures?
2 Which room is your favorite? Why?

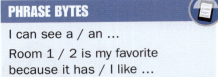

PHRASE BYTES

I can see a / an …

Room 1 / 2 is my favorite because it has / I like …

Room 1

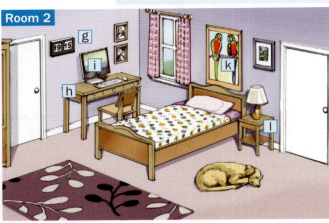

Room 2

2 a Match the things in the pictures (a–l) to the words in the box.

bed *e*	chair ___	clock ___	computer ___	desk ___	door ___
floor ___	light ___	picture ___	table ___	wall ___	window ___

b ▶1.47 Listen and check. Then listen and repeat.

3 Write the words from Exercise 2a in the correct category.

Parts of a room: *door, …*   **Other things:** *clock, …*
Furniture: *bed, …*

SPEAK AND LISTEN

4 ▶1.48 Listen to the conversation. Which room is it, Room 1 or Room 2?

5 a ▶1.48 Answer the questions. Then listen again. Compare your answers with a partner.

1 Who's talking – people or pet animals?
2 Who's the new neighbor – a boy, a girl, a cat, or a dog?
3 What happens at the end?

b Look at page 115 to check your answers.

6 a Complete the sentences with words from Exercise 2.

"Of course there's a (1) ___*window*___ . You're looking in it!"
"There's a small (2) _____ next to the bed with a (3) _____ on it."
"There are some (4) _____ on the walls."
"There are two (5) _____ . And there's a (6) _____ with a computer."
"Is he there?" – "Yes! He's on the (7) _____ ."

b ▶1.49 Listen and check your answers.

REACT

7 Work in pairs. Ask and answer.

1 What's your favorite room in your house?
2 What things are in that room?

PHRASE BYTES

My favorite room is …

There's a / an …

MOVE BEYOND

Do the Words & Beyond exercise on page 108.

>>> **Describe a room**

READ AND LISTEN >>> Grammar in context

1 ▶1.50 **Read and listen to the conversation. What's wrong with the computer room?**

Natalie: What's your English classroom like?
Mario: It's OK. There's a table and a chair for the teacher. There are desks for the students. There are some windows. Oh, and there are some pictures of the USA and the UK on the wall, but there isn't a picture of Australia.
Natalie: Is there a clock?
Mario: Yes, there is. It's next to the door. Why?
Natalie: The questions are for a school survey. Are there any computers?
Mario: No, there aren't. There are computers in the computer room. I don't like the computer room. There aren't any windows.

STUDY

2 a Complete the table. Use Exercise 1 to help you.

There is / there are
Use *there is / there are* to describe what's in a place.

Affirmative	Negative
There's a table.	There **isn't** a picture of Australia.
There **are** (some) desks.	There _____ **any** computers.

Questions	Short answers
Is there a clock?	Yes, there _____ . / No, there isn't.
Are there any computers?	Yes, there are. / No, there _____ .

See **GRAMMAR DATABASE**, page 100.

b Underline **examples of** *there is / there are* **in Exercise 1.**

PRACTICE

3 Look at the picture of Mario's computer room. Are the sentences correct (*C*) or incorrect (*I*)? Rewrite the incorrect sentences.

1 There are some windows. *I*
   There aren't any windows.
2 There are some brown chairs.
3 There's a clock on the wall.
4 There's one door.
5 There aren't any pictures on the walls.
6 There are three computers.

4 Write questions about your classroom. Then ask and answer them.

1 (a clock) *Is there a clock?*
2 (windows) _____
3 (a table for your teacher) _____
4 (pictures on the wall) _____
5 (a bed) _____
6 (computers) _____

5 Complete the conversation with the correct form of *there is / there are*.

Natalie: What's your room like?
Mario: OK. (1) *There's* a bed and a table.
Natalie: (2) _____ a computer on the table?
Mario: No, (3) _____ .
Natalie: (4) _____ any pictures on the walls?
Mario: Yes, there are. (5) _____ some pictures of my favorite soccer team.
Natalie: Is there a window?
Mario: Yes, (6) _____ .

SPEAK

6 Work in pairs. Complete the tasks.

- Draw a plan of your room and the things in your room. Don't show it to your partner.
- Ask questions about your partner's room. Make a list of his/her things.
- Compare your list with your partner's plan.

Is there a/an … in your room?

Are there any … ?

Yes, there is/are.

No, there isn't/aren't.

LANGUAGE &BEYOND

>>> **Prepare your things for school**

SPEAK AND READ

1 a 🔊 **Work in pairs. Look at the pictures for one minute. Then close your books and write the things you remember.**

b **Open your books and check your lists.**

2 **Work in pairs. Which desk is it (A, B, or A and B)?**

1 It's before school. *A and B*
2 The desk is neat. _____
3 The homework isn't finished. _____
4 This person's ready for school. _____

DO

3 a **Do you usually do these things before bed (A) or before school (B)? Circle your answers.**

Do homework	A / B	Ask for bus money	A / B
Prepare clothes for school	A / B	Prepare lunch	A / B
Pack your backpack	A / B	Find keys	A / B

b **Where do you usually keep these things – on a table, in your pocket, or in your backpack?**

school books   keys   money   pens   phone

4 **Work in pairs. Compare your answers to Exercises 3a and 3b. When is the best time to do the things in Exercise 3a? Are the places in Exercise 3b good or bad?**

It's good to keep your phone in …
It's bad to keep your money …

REFLECT

5 🗣 **Talk about the questions. Then read the** REFLECTION POINT.

1 When is it good to prepare your school things and do homework?
2 Is it good to keep your school things in one place or different places?
3 Are you ready for school in the morning?

EXTEND

6 **Work in groups. Think of three tips to help students organize their things at school and be ready for each class.**

It's good to … / It isn't good to …   *Keep your things …*

REFLECTION POINT

It's good to prepare your school things and do homework before you go to bed. It's good to keep your school things in a special place. You can find them quickly and not be late for school.

SCHOOL SKILLS

>>>> Workbook, page 41

>>> **Ask for and give things**

SPEAK

1 🔊 **Work in pairs. What things can you see in the pictures?**

LISTEN

2 a **Complete the conversations and write the missing words. Use the pictures to help you.**

> **1**
> **Jeff:** Can I have some (1) _____ , please?
> **Lisa:** Yes, of course. Here you are.
> **Jeff:** Thanks.
> **Lisa:** You're welcome.

> **2**
> **Mia:** Excuse me. Can I borrow your (2) _____ ?
> **Brett:** Sure. Here you are.
> **Mia:** Thanks.
> **Brett:** You're welcome.

> **3**
> **Amy:** Hi, Kevin. Can I borrow your (3) _____ ?
> **Kevin:** No, sorry.
> **Amy:** Oh. OK.
> **Donna:** You can borrow mine.
> **Amy:** Thanks, Donna.
> **Donna:** You're welcome.

b ▶1.51 **Listen to the conversations and check your answers.**

3 **Complete the sentences with *have* and *borrow*.**

  1 If you ask to _____ something, you don't keep it.
  2 If you ask to _____ something, you keep it.

4 ▶1.52 **Listen and repeat.**

5 ▶1.53 **Put the sentences in order to make a conversation between Kevin and his dad. Then listen and check.**

  _____ Please, Dad!
  _____ OK. Here you are.
  _____ No, sorry.
  _____ Thank you.
  _____ Dad? Can I have some money?
  _____ You're welcome.

ACT

6 🔊 **Work in pairs. Complete the tasks.**

- Prepare two conversations – one at school and one at home.
- Use *borrow* in one conversation and *have* in the other.
- Present your conversations to other students.

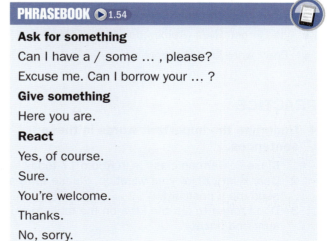

PHRASEBOOK ▶1.54

Ask for something

Can I have a / some … , please?

Excuse me. Can I borrow your … ?

Give something

Here you are.

React

Yes, of course.

Sure.

You're welcome.

Thanks.

No, sorry.

WRITING **Don't forget**

READ

1 Match the notes to the pictures.

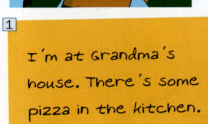

1 I'm at Grandma's house. There's some pizza in the kitchen. Be good. Mom.

2 Don't forget! Give Harry some food and water. There's cat food on the table. Sue.

3 William!! Call Barbara before 4 p.m. Basketball practice is at 6 p.m. Dad.

2 Read the notes again and answer the questions.

1. Where's Mom?
2. What's for lunch?
3. Who or what is Harry?
4. Where's Harry's food?
5. Who is Dad's note for?
6. What time is basketball practice?

3 Read the tips in the HOW TO box. Then circle the imperatives in the three notes.

HOW TO ?

write a note

- Write important information.
- Use imperatives (*Remember / Don't forget ...*).
- Don't write long sentences.

PRACTICE

4 <u>Underline</u> the important words in these sentences.

1. Class C: German class is in Room 17 today.
2. Dear Hilary, Enjoy your vacation. Please write and send me a postcard.
3. Don't forget to put the keys on the table for your aunt and uncle.

DISCUSS

5 Talk about work you do at home. Do you help make dinner? Do you feed the dog or cat? Talk about instructions your parents give you to do the job.

WRITE

6 Write a note to give instructions to a family member or friend.

1. Who is the person you are writing to? What instructions does the person need? Is your note about your pet, a school activity, or food?
2. Write your note using imperatives. Remember to start with *Don't* to tell the person not to do something.
3. Write a short note. Don't add information that is not important. Read the tips in the HOW TO box.

SHARE

7 Read your note to other students. Vote on who had the clearest instructions.

VOCABULARY Pet animals

1 Write the words for the pets.

1 d _____
2 r _____
3 c _____
4 m _____
5 b _____
6 t _____
7 h _____
8 c _____
9 f _____
10 h _____

___ /10

Things in your room

2 Choose the correct options to complete the text.

HOME ABOUT RESERVATIONS

All our rooms have four (1) *clocks / walls* , a (2) *door / floor* (with a special key), a big (3) *bed / window* to look at the street, and a (4) *floor / picture* (if you don't sleep in a bed).

There's a big (5) *bed / table* to sleep on (if you don't like the floor). There's a small (6) *light / table* next to the bed with a (7) *light / table* on it. If you want the internet, sit on the (8) *chair / computer* at the (9) *desk / door* and use the (10) *computer / window* . It's free!

What time is it? Look at the (11) *clock / picture* on the wall. There's also a (12) *table / picture* of me on the wall. Have a nice stay!

___ /12

GRAMMAR Imperatives and object pronouns

3 Complete the text with the words and phrases in the box.

come	don't forget	don't stay	eat	him
them	us	you		

Pet Hotel   HOME ABOUT RESERVATIONS

Are you an animal? (1) _____ in a normal hotel. (2) _____ to the Pet Hotel! At the Pet Hotel, we really understand (3) _____ . (4) _____ in the Pet Hotel's famous restaurant. Talk to our chef, Mr. Rex, and tell (5) _____ your favorite food. Make new animal friends and relax with (6) _____ in our yard. (7) _____ the name – the Pet Hotel. Call (8) _____ now at 1-800-PET-HOTEL!

___ /16

There is / there are

4 Match the sentence halves.

Pet Hotel   HOME ABOUT RESERVATIONS

Any questions?
1 Is there _____
2 Yes, _____
3 There's a _____
4 Are there any _____
5 No. There aren't any _____
6 There are some _____

a big yard with a lot of grass.
b people at the hotel.
c there is.
d a yard?
e birds, dogs, cats, and one elephant.
f people at the Pet Hotel?

___ / 12

Your score: ___ / 50

SKILLS CHECK

✓✓✓	Yes, I can. No problem!
✓✓	Yes, I can. But I need a little help.
✓	Yes, I can. But I need a lot of help.

I can read instructions. _____
I can listen to a description of a room. _____
I can prepare my things for school. _____
I can ask for and give things. _____
I can write a note. _____

»»» Workbook, pages 42–43

IN THE PICTURE Free time

>>> Talk about your free-time activities

WORK WITH WORDS Free-time activities

1 **RECALL** Work in pairs. Find 10 "free-time" words and phrases. You have three minutes. (Clue: Look at the pictures for help.)

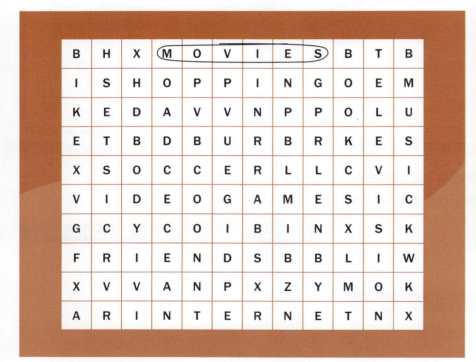

B	H	X	M	O	V	I	E	S	B	T	B
I	S	H	O	P	P	I	N	G	O	E	M
K	E	D	A	V	V	N	P	P	O	L	U
E	T	B	D	B	U	R	B	R	K	E	S
X	S	O	C	C	E	R	L	L	C	V	I
V	I	D	E	O	G	A	M	E	S	I	C
G	C	Y	C	O	I	B	I	N	X	S	K
F	R	I	E	N	D	S	B	B	L	I	W
X	V	V	A	N	P	X	Z	Y	M	O	K
A	R	I	N	T	E	R	N	E	T	N	X

2 ▶2.01 Work in pairs. Complete the free-time activities with the words in Exercise 1. Listen and check. Then listen and repeat.

1 go *shopping*
2 go to the _____
3 go on the _____
4 listen to _____
5 meet _____
6 play _____
7 play _____
8 read a _____
9 ride my _____
10 watch _____

3 ▶2.02 Listen to Jade. Match her free-time activities to the pictures (a–j).

4 **THE MOVING PICTURE** ▶ Watch the video and write the free-time activities.

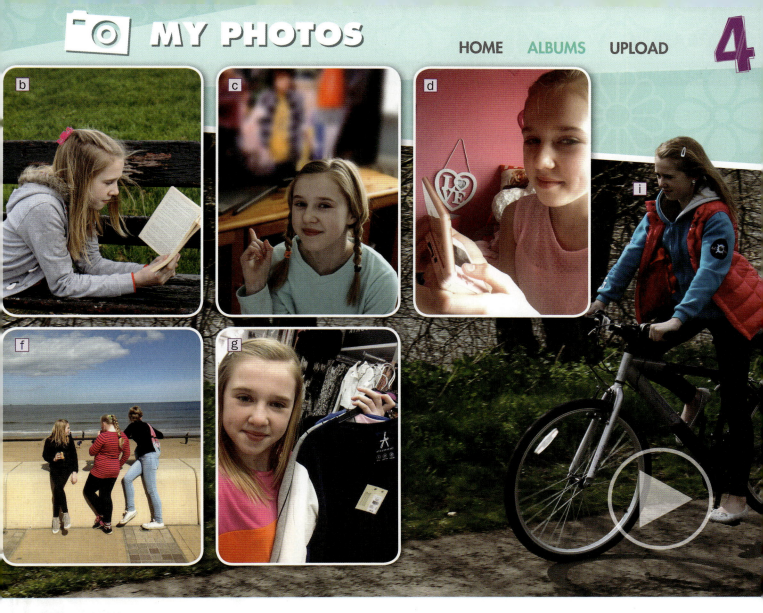

WRITE AND SPEAK

5 a Complete the chart with your top five free-time activities from Exercise 2.

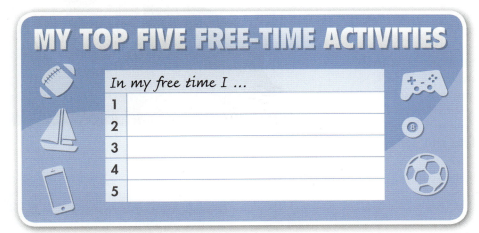

MY TOP FIVE FREE-TIME ACTIVITIES

In my free time I ...

1
2
3
4
5

b Work in pairs. Compare your top five activities.

What's your number one / next activity?

My number two / next activity is ...

That's my favorite too.

Really? Mine is ...

MOVE BEYOND

Do the Words & Beyond exercise on page 109.

>>> Read an article on a website

SPEAK AND READ

1 Work in pairs. Match the disabilities to the pictures.

.... blind .... deaf .... in a wheelchair

2 Look at the website article. Answer the questions.

1 Who's the boy in the picture?
2 Where's he from?
3 What's his disability?

WE CAN! A look at the lives of children with disabilities

Home   News   Articles   About

A message from Jason ▼

The WE CAN! interview

Name: Jason Collins
Home: Miami, Florida, the United States

Hi, Jason. Can you hear me?
I can, but please sit in front of me.

How much can you hear?
I can't hear in my right ear. In my left ear I'm 50 percent deaf, but my hearing aid helps.

What's it like for a deaf boy at school?
It's OK. Sometimes people say bad things when they see my hearing aid. They think I can't do normal things. But I can play soccer, watch TV – all the things they can do.

You write a very popular blog. Why is it popular?
Because when people read it, they can understand my problems. It's not easy for a deaf person in a noisy world.

Can you use sign language?
Yes, I can. I use sign language with a deaf girl at school.

Can other students understand you?
No, they can't! But they can say, *Hi, how are you?* and *I'm fine* in sign language!

3 ▶2.03 Read the article. Complete the sentences with TWO words.

1 He's completely deaf in his ....
2 There's a .... in his left ear.
3 Jason's deaf, but he can do ....
4 His blog is ....
5 The blog is about the life of a .... in a noisy world.
6 He talks to a deaf girl at his school in ....

4 a Look at the pictures in the article. What's Jason saying?

b Work in pairs. Practice the sign language.

REACT

5 💬 Work in pairs. What do you think? Tell your partner.

Jason says, "It's not easy for a deaf person in a noisy world." What things do you think are difficult for a deaf person?

>>> Workbook, page 45

>>> **Talk about the things you can do**

READ AND LISTEN >>> Grammar in context

1 ▶ 2.04 **Read and listen to the conversation. What's Maya's disability?**

Jan: Can you pass me an orange, please?
Maya: I'm sorry, I can't see them.
Jan: Oh? Are you blind?
Maya: Yes, but I can see some things.
Jan: Can you see me?
Maya: Yes, I can, but I can't see your face. Most blind people can see light and dark things. But my teacher's completely blind. She can't see anything.

STUDY

2 **Complete the examples. Use Exercise 1 to help you.**

Can/can't	
Affirmative	**Negative**
I __can__ see some things.	I __can't__ see your face.
They _____ see light and dark things.	She _____ see anything.
Questions	**Short answers**
__Can__ you _____ me?	Yes, I __can__ .
_____ your teacher see your face?	No, she _____ .

See GRAMMAR DATABASE, page 101.

PRACTICE

3 **Choose the correct options about Maya in Exercise 1.**

1 Maya (can) / can't see people.
2 She *can* / *can't* watch television.
3 She *can* / *can't* read normal books.
4 She *can* / *can't* listen to audio books.
5 Her teacher *can* / *can't* see people.

4 a **Work in pairs. What do you think Mateo can do? Write sentences with *He can* and *He can't*.**

1 swim
2 walk
3 take the bus
4 ride a bike
5 play soccer
6 play basketball

b ▶ 2.05 **Listen to Mateo and check your answers.**

5 a **Put the words in order to make questions.**

1 swim? / you / Can
  Can you swim?
2 Can / yes in German? / you / say
3 tennis? / Can / play / your teacher
4 people / in New Zealand / English? / Can / speak
5 with your foot? / you / touch your head / Can
6 you and your classmates / for 10 minutes? / be / Can / quiet

b **Answer the questions. Use short answers.**

1 *Yes, I can. / No, I can't.*

SPEAK

6 **Work in groups of three. Ask questions with *can*. Find:**

- three things that you can all do.
- one thing that you can do and your partners can't.

Can you ride a bike?

What languages can you speak?

»» **Listen to street interviews**

WORK WITH WORDS Music

1 ▶2.06 **Match the instruments to the pictures. Listen and check. Then listen and repeat.**

| _____ drums | _____ guitar | _____ keyboard | _____ piano | _____ violin |

2 a ▶2.07 **Work in pairs. Listen and match the pieces of music (1–5) to the types of music in the box.**

| _____ classical | _____ hip-hop | _____ Latin | _____ pop | _____ rock |

b ▶2.08 **Listen and check. Then listen and repeat.**

3 a ▶2.09 **PRONOUNCE** **Listen and repeat the /v/ sound in _violin_.**

b ▶2.10 **Listen and repeat these words.**

video   movie   interview   television

4 🔲 **Work in pairs. Ask and answer.**

1 Can you play an instrument? → YES: What instrument?
                                   NO: What instruments do you like?

2 Can you sing or dance?
3 What kind of music do you like?

LISTEN

5 ▶2.11 **Listen to three interviews. Are the people musical? Write _Yes_ or _No_.**

Dora _____   Penny _____   Neil _____   Rianna _____

6 ▶2.11 **Listen again. Complete the sentences with names from Exercise 5.**

1 _____ writes songs.
2 _____ doesn't like pop music.
3 _____ can dance.
4 _____ likes classical music.
5 _____ likes Latin music.
6 _____ and _____ play an instrument.

REACT

7 🔲 **Work in groups. Are _you_ musical? Explain why.**

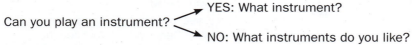

PHRASE BYTES

I can play the …
I like the …
I like … music / hip-hop.

PHRASE BYTES

I think / don't think I'm …
I'm definitely not …
I'm not sure.
I can / can't …

MOVE BEYOND **»**

Do the Words & Beyond exercise on page 109.

>>> **Talk about habits and routines**

READ AND LISTEN >>> Grammar in context

1 ▶2.12 **Read and listen to the interview. What's special about the group?**

TV host: Hello. On today's show we have The Wilsons. Jackie, tell us about your music.

Jackie: Well, we play pop music, but it has a traditional sound too. I play the guitar and I sing. My sister plays the violin. She teaches the violin too. That's my brother Max on keyboards. He writes our songs. And this is a new song. It goes like this …

STUDY

2 **Complete the examples. Use Exercise 1 to help you.**

Simple Present
Affirmative
Use the base verb for *I, you, we, they.*
I   *play*   the guitar.
We   pop music.
They play different instruments.
Use the verb + -s/-es for *he, she, it.*
He   *writes*   our songs.
My sister   the violin.
It   like this.
She   the violin too.
Irregular Verb
It   a traditional sound too.

See GRAMMAR DATABASE, page 101.

PRACTICE

3 **Write the verb + -s, -es, or -ies.**

	verb	he/she/it		verb	he/she/it
1	listen	*listens*	5	practice	
2	watch		6	do	
3	read		7	study	
4	talk		8	arrive	

4 **Complete the descriptions with the verbs in Exercise 3.**

The La teens
home   about   free time

Free time

Carlos is quiet. In his free time he
(1)   *reads*   a lot of books and he
(2)   to his friends on the internet.
He also (3)   to a lot of different
kinds of music – pop, rock, hip-hop, and
classical.

Sofia's crazy about music. She (4)
music at a music school three days a week
after school, and when she (5)
home, she (6)   the piano for hours.

Juan's very active. He (7)   a lot of
different activities in his free time. He's also
a big soccer fan. He (8)   soccer
games on television on weekends.

5 **Complete the message with the simple present form of the verbs.**

The La teens
LIKE   FOLLOW

Hi! We're The Lateens, and we (1)   *live*
(**live**) in Santiago, the capital city of Chile. We
(2)   (**play**) Latin pop music with hip-hop
influences. My name's Sofia, and I'm the singer.
I (3)   (**come**) from a musical family.
My mother (4)   (**teach**) piano. Carlos
(5)   (**play**) the guitar and keyboard. His
guitar hero is Jimi Hendrix, and he (6)
(**copy**) all his solos. Juan plays the drums. Our
group only (7)   (**have**) three members,
so for concerts, we (8)   (**invite**) other
people to play with us.

WRITE AND SPEAK

6 a **Work in pairs. Write two or three sentences about a famous group or singer. Don't write the name.**

b **Work with another pair.**

- Tell the other pair about your famous group or singer. (Don't read your sentences.)
- Listen and write the name of the other pair's singer or group.
- At the end, check your answers.

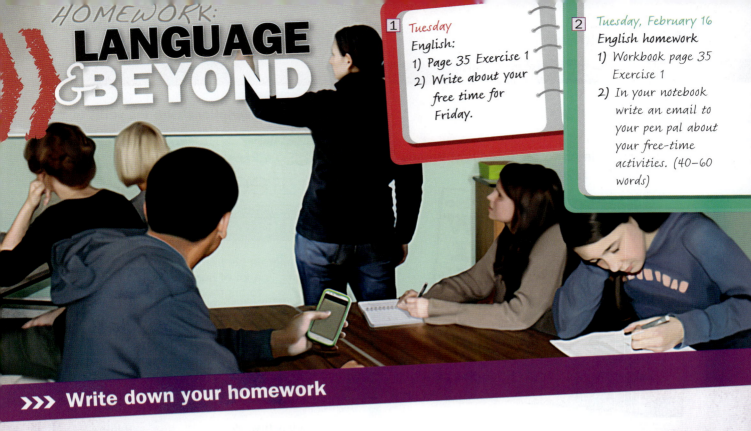

1 Tuesday
English:
1) Page 35 Exercise 1
2) Write about your free time for Friday.

2 Tuesday, February 16
English homework
1) Workbook page 35 Exercise 1
2) In your notebook write an email to your pen pal about your free-time activities. (40–60 words)

>>> Write down your homework

SCHOOL SKILLS

SPEAK AND READ

1 Choose the correct option for you. Then compare with a partner.

1 I get *a little* / *a lot of* homework.
2 I get homework *two or three* / *three or four* / *five* days a week.
3 I do my homework at *home* / *school* .

2 a Read the lists. Then check (✓) the things you can see in the picture.

How teachers can give homework:
Write it on the board.
Tell students.
Put it on the school website.

How students can write down homework:
Make a note on a phone.
Write it on a piece of paper.
Write it in a homework planner.

b 🔊 Work in pairs. Ask and answer the questions.

1 How do your teachers give homework?
2 How do you write it down?

DO

3 Work in pairs. Look at the homework planners above. Then answer the questions.

1 Which homework planner answers these questions (1, 2, or both)?
   a What is the homework?
   b What books do I need?
   c Where do I write it?
   d When is it due?
2 Which planner has more information about the homework?

REFLECT

4 🔊 Talk about the questions. Then read the (REFLECTION POINT).

1 Can you always remember your homework?
2 Is your homework always ready on time?
3 What's the best way to remember homework? Give details.

EXTEND

5 Make a note of your English homework in English. For help, look again at planner 2 in Exercise 3.

PHRASE BYTES

Our English teacher writes / tells …

I write it down in / on …

I write it …

PHRASE BYTES

Yes, I can. / No, I can't.

Not always, but …

The best way is to …

REFLECTION POINT «

It's important to write down your homework. Always ask: *What's the task? What do I need? Where do I do it? When is it due?*

>>> Workbook, page 53

>>> **Tell the time**

SPEAK

1 🗣 Work in pairs. Look at the picture. What can you see? Where are Kelly and Mike?

LISTEN

2 ▶2.13 **Listen to the conversations. What do they decide to do at the end?**

1
Mike: What time is the movie?
Kelly: It's at seven o'clock.
Mike: What time is it now?
Kelly: It's a quarter after six.
Mike: We have time.

2
Mike: Kelly? What time is it?
Kelly: It's six thirty.
Mike: Six thirty? The bus is late!

3
Mike: Kelly? What time is it now?
Kelly: It's six thirty-five.
Mike: Twenty-five to seven? Oh no! Where's the bus?

4
Mike: Kelly? What time is it?
Kelly: It's a quarter to seven. Let's go home.
Mike: Good idea.

3 **Read the conversations. Write the times under the clocks.**

1 *seven o'clock* 2 _____ 3 _____ 4 _____ 5 _____

4 ▶2.14 **Listen and repeat the questions and the times.**

5 a **Draw clocks with these times. Use Exercise 3 and the picture to help you.**

1 It's five o'clock.
2 It's ten to twelve.
3 It's a quarter after nine.
4 It's eleven thirty.
5 It's a quarter to four.
6 It's twenty-five past six.

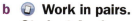
to — after/past

b 🗣 **Work in pairs.**
Student A: close your book.
Student B: point to a clock and ask the time. Repeat for the other clocks. Then change roles.

ACT

6 🗣 **Work in pairs. Complete the tasks.**

■ Write a conversation between two people before a movie, concert, or exam. Include two time questions and two times.
■ Practice your conversation. Then present it to other students.

WRITING My free time

>>> Write an email

SPEAK AND READ

1 🔊 **Work in pairs. Circle the correct options for you. Compare your answers.**

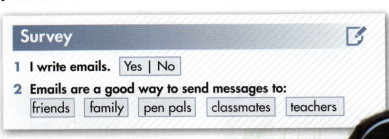

Survey	✏️
1 I write emails. Yes | No	
2 Emails are a good way to send messages to: friends | family | pen pals | classmates | teachers	

2 **Read the email. Who's Clara?**

✉️ New mail ← Reply → Forward

Hi Clara,

It's great to have a new pen pal in Argentina. I can't speak Spanish, so we can practice our English. You ask about my free time. Well, I meet my friends, go shopping, and go on the internet. On Mondays I have a guitar class. My sister teaches me too. She plays in a group.

Write soon,

Greta

3 **Read the tips in the HOW TO box. Then circle other examples of capital letters in the email.**

HOW TO ❓
use capital letters

- Use at the start of a new sentence: *It's great to … .*
- Use for the pronoun "I": *I have a guitar class.*
- Use for the names of people and places: *Hi Clara.*
- Use for countries, nationalities, and languages: *Argentina, Spanish.*
- Use for days of the week: *Monday.*
- Use at the start of an email message: *Dear, Hi.*
- Use at the end of an email message: *Write soon.*

PRACTICE

4 **Rewrite the email with capital letters.**

hi greta,

thanks for your email. it's great to have a pen pal in germany. is german difficult? i think i'm a typical teenager. i meet my friends in my free time too. on saturdays we go to the movies. at home i listen to music, but i can't play an instrument.

best wishes,
clara

DISCUSS

5 **Talk about your free-time activities. What do you do after school or on the weekend? Can you play a musical instrument or a special sport? Do you have special lessons or activities on one day of the week?**

WRITE

6 **Write an email to a pen pal who lives in another country.**

1 Write to your pen pal about things you normally do outside of school. Write about special things you can do.

2 Use verbs in the simple present to write about activities you normally do. Use *can* for special things you know how to do. Remember to use *don't* and *can't* in negative sentences.

3 Use capital letters correctly. See the HOW TO box and check your email for errors.

SHARE

7 **Take turns reading your descriptions. Listen to your classmates. Are your free-time activities different or the same?**

VOCABULARY Free-time activities

1 Complete the ad with the words in the box.

> a book   friends   music   my bike
> shopping   soccer   television   the internet
> the movies   video games

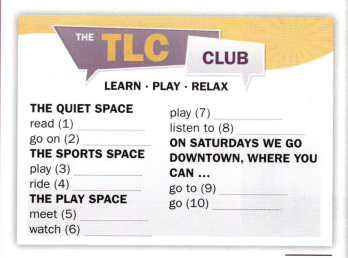

THE TLC CLUB

LEARN · PLAY · RELAX

THE QUIET SPACE
read (1) _____
go on (2) _____
THE SPORTS SPACE
play (3) _____
ride (4) _____
THE PLAY SPACE
meet (5) _____
watch (6) _____

play (7) _____
listen to (8) _____
ON SATURDAYS WE GO DOWNTOWN, WHERE YOU CAN ...
go to (9) _____
go (10) _____

___ /10

Music

2 Complete the words.

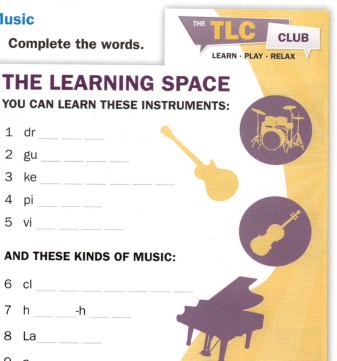

THE TLC CLUB

LEARN · PLAY · RELAX

THE LEARNING SPACE

YOU CAN LEARN THESE INSTRUMENTS:

1 dr _____
2 gu _____
3 ke _____
4 pi _____
5 vi _____

AND THESE KINDS OF MUSIC:

6 cl _____
7 h _____ -h _____
8 La _____
9 p _____
10 r _____

___ /10

GRAMMAR Can/can't

3 Complete the interview with *can/can't* and the words in parentheses.

Lou: (1) _____ (I/study) music at the TLC?

Dina: Yes, you (2) _____ . We have a fantastic teacher. She (3) _____ (play) five instruments. (4) _____ (you/play) an instrument?

Lou: No, I (5) _____ . But I want to sing. (6) _____ (she/teach) me to sing?

Dina: Oh yes. But are you free on Tuesdays or Thursdays? She (7) _____ (not come) on other days.

Lou: I (8) _____ (be) here on Thursdays.

Dina: Great! See you next Thursday, then.

___ /16

Simple present

4 Complete the email with the simple present form of the verbs.

> ✉ New mail   ← Reply   → Forward   ⊗
>
> Hi Ursula,
> How are you? I have a new free-time activity! I (1) _____ (go) to singing classes. The teacher's name is Helen. She (2) _____ (come) from Russia. She (3) _____ (study) music at the Music School, and she (4) _____ (teach) in the afternoon. We (5) _____ (have) class on Thursday when school (6) _____ (finish). My friends (7) _____ (want) to take classes too!
> Write soon,
> Lou

___ /14

Your score: ___ /50

SKILLS CHECK

> ✓✓✓ Yes, I can. No problem!
> ✓✓ Yes, I can. But I need a little help.
> ✓ Yes, I can. But I need a lot of help.

I can read an article on a website. _____
I can listen to street interviews. _____
I can make a clear note of my homework. _____
I can tell the time. _____
I can write an email. _____

READ

1 Read the sentences about Oliver's free time. Choose the best word (A, B, or C) for each blank.

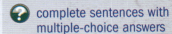

TEST-TAKING TIPS

? complete sentences with multiple-choice answers

- Look at the example.
- Read each sentence and the choices (A, B, or C).
- Decide which words are wrong. For each word, check:
  – Does it have the correct meaning?
  – Can you use it with the words before and after it?
- Read the sentence again. Check your answer.

Example:

0 In the evening I _____ television.
   A look   **B** see   **Ⓒ** watch

---

1 After school I go on the _____ .
   A internet   **B** movies   **C** shopping

2 I listen _____ music on my phone.
   A at   **B** with   **C** to

3 My favorite kind _____ music is Latin.
   A in   **B** of   **C** at

4 I can play the _____ .
   A soccer   **B** piano   **C** video games

5 I _____ my friends on weekends.
   A play   **B** listen   **C** meet

Reading: _____ /10

LISTEN

2 **2.16** **Listen to Delia and Luke. What animals or pets do the people in Delia's family have? For questions 1–5, write the correct letter (A–H) next to each person.**

Example:

0   Mom   *B*

PEOPLE		PETS	
1 Dad		A bird	E mouse
2 her brother		B cat	F fish
3 her sister		C chickens	G horse
4 Grandma		D dog	H hamster
5 Grandpa			

Listening: _____ /10

WRITE

3 **Complete Alice's email to her friend. For questions 1–10, write one word for each blank.**

Example:

0   *for*

✉ New mail   ← Reply   → Forward   ✕

Dear Lucia,
Thanks (0) _*for*_ your email about your free time. On school days
I (1) _____ homework after school. On weekends I (2) _____
my bike or I (3) _____ shopping with my mom. I have (4) _____
dog. Her name's Cookie. I take (5) _____ to the park at a quarter
(6) _____ seven every morning. She's old and a little deaf, so she
(7) _____ hear me. But she's a smart dog. She (8) _____ play
soccer! Do you (9) _____ a pet?
(10) _____ soon!
Alice

Writing: _____ / 10

Progress check score _____ /30

UNIT 5

OTHER WORLDS

IN THE PICTURE Welcome to Tomorrowtown

>>> **Talk about jobs**

WORK WITH WORDS Jobs

1 **RECALL** Work in pairs. Write the places. You have two minutes.

1 f _____

5 s _____ stadium

2 h _____

6 h _____

3 r _____

7 s _____

4 s _____

8 t _____

2 a Match the people (a–j) in the picture to the places (1–8) in Exercise 1.

  1–g

 b ▶2.17 Listen and check who the people are and where they work.

3 a Complete the sentences with the jobs in the box.

> actor   cook   doctor   farmer   nurse   receptionist
> sales clerk   soccer player   teacher   waiter/waitress

1 "Hi. I'm a(n) _____ . I work at the Tomorrowtown hospital."
2 "I work at the hospital with the doctor. I'm a(n) _____ ."
3 "Hello. I'm a(n) _____ . You can see me at the Tomorrowtown Theater."
4 "Welcome to Tomorrowtown Hotel. I'm a(n) _____ at the hotel."
5 "I'm a(n) _____ . My farm is two kilometers from here."
6 "I'm a(n) _____ in a clothing store. There are a lot of stores in Tomorrowtown."
7 "I'm a(n) _____ at Tomorrowtown's Italian restaurant."
8 "We work at the Italian restaurant. I'm a(n) _____ and he's a(n) _____ ."
9 "I'm a(n) _____ . People come to see me play at Tomorrowtown Soccer Stadium."
10 "I'm a(n) _____ at Tomorrowtown High School. I teach all the kids in Tomorrowtown."

 b ▶2.18 Listen and check. Then listen and repeat.

WELCOME TO TOMORROWTOWN
your virtual home on the web

5

4 a ▶ 2.19 **PRONOUNCE** Listen and repeat the /ər/ sound in these words.

doct<u>or</u>   farm<u>er</u>   teach<u>er</u>

b ▶ 2.20 Find three more jobs in Exercise 3 with the /ər/ sound. Then listen and check.

5 **THE MOVING PICTURE** ▶ Watch the video about Tomorrowtown. Which job in Exercise 3a is NOT in the video?

SPEAK

6 Work in pairs. Read and follow the Tomorrowtown instructions.

Hi. My name's … I'm a/an …

Hello, Alex. I'm … I'm a/an …

I work in …

7 Introduce yourself to other students in the class. What are their jobs? Which is the class's favorite job?

WELCOME TO
TOMORROWTOWN

1 Look at the Tomorrowtown people. Choose a person. *Tip:* Choose a different person from your partner.
2 Answer these questions: *What's your name? What's your job?*
3 Introduce yourself to your partner.

MOVE BEYOND ››

Do the Words & Beyond exercise on page 110.

››› Workbook, page 56

>>> Read a questionnaire

SPEAK AND READ

1 Work in pairs. Ask and answer.

1 How old are you? What do you do?
2 Go 15 years into the future. How old are you? What do you do?

2 ▶2.21 **Read the instructions for the questionnaire. Decide if the sentences are correct (C) or incorrect (I). Correct the incorrect sentences.**

1 The questionnaire helps you find the perfect type of job for you. ....
2 For each question, you can choose one or two answers. ....
3 You check (✓) the answers you choose. ....
4 When you finish, you count your answers (A, B, or C). ....
5 If your answers are 1A, 2C, and 3A, you read the section *Mostly As*. ....

3 **Complete the questionnaire and read your results.**

My perfect job

Instructions

Find your perfect job of the future. Read each question and circle **one** of the answers, A, B, or C. Then count the number of A, B, or C answers and read about your perfect job.

What your score means

Mostly As
You like people. Your perfect job is a doctor, nurse, sales clerk, or receptionist.

Mostly Bs
You're an active person. Your perfect job is a farmer or soccer player.

Mostly Cs
You like to create. Your perfect job is an actor, cook, or teacher.

1 Which of these free-time activities do you do?
A I meet friends or go shopping.
B I play soccer or ride my bike.
C I go to the movies or read a book.

2 Which musical instrument do you want to play?
A I want to play the guitar in a pop group.
B I want to play the drums.
C I want to play the piano and sing.

3 Do you play games?
A Yes, I do. I play video games with my friends.
B Yes, I do. I play ball games such as soccer and basketball.
C No, I don't. I like to make things.

4 **Add *waiter/waitress* to one of the groups. Which group is the best (A, B, or C)?**

REACT

5 Work in pairs. Ask and answer the questions.

1 Do you agree with the results of the questionnaire?
2 Is your perfect job in the questionnaire?
3 Do you like questionnaires? Why or why not?

 Workbook, page 57

GRAMMAR Simple present

>>> Ask and answer questions about habits and routines

READ AND LISTEN >>> Grammar in context

1 a Read the questions and answers. Where does the mystery person work? What's her job?

Q: Does the mystery person work on a farm?
A: No, she doesn't.
Q: Does she work in a hotel?
A: Yes, she does. But she isn't a receptionist.
Q: What time does she start work?
A: I don't know.
Q: Does she work in the hotel restaurant?
A: Yes, she does. But she doesn't cook.
Q: Do people ask her for things?
A: Yes, they do.
Q: What do they ask her for?
A: They ask her for food.
Q: Is she a _____ ?
A: Yes, she is.

b ▶2.22 Listen and check.

STUDY

2 Complete the examples. Use Exercise 1 to help you.

Simple Present		
Affirmative		**Negative**
I know.		*I* ___don't___ *know.*
She cooks.		*She* _____ *cook.*
Questions and short answers		
___Do___ *you know the answer?*		
Yes, I ___do___ *. / No, I* ___don't___ *.*		
_____ *she* _____ *in a hotel?*		
Yes, she _____ *. / No, she* _____ *.*		
_____ *people ask her for things?*		
Yes, they _____ *. / No, they don't.*		
Question words		
_____ *time does she start work?*		
_____ *do they ask her for?*		

See GRAMMAR DATABASE, page 102.

PRACTICE

3 a Complete the sentences with the correct form of the verbs.

| ask | buy | do | give | help |
| smile | watch | ~~work~~ | | |

1 I ___work___ with animals.
2 People _____ things from me.
3 The waiter _____ my food to people.
4 You _____ me play soccer.
5 I _____ people.
6 Your teacher _____ the same job.
7 I _____ : "Would you like to order now?"
8 I _____ at people in a hotel.

b ▶2.23 Make the sentences negative. Listen and check. Then identify the mystery job.

1 *I don't work with animals.*

4 Complete the conversation with *do*, *don't*, *does*, or *doesn't*.

Mollie: (1) ___Do___ you know Jenny?
Jane: No, I (2) _____ .
(3) _____ she go to our school?
Mollie: Yes, she (4) _____ . She says her mom and dad are famous.
Jane: Really? What (5) _____ they do?
Mollie: Her dad's a soccer player, and her mom's an actor.
Jane: Wow! Who are they?
Mollie: I (6) _____ know. It's a mystery.
Jane: (7) _____ you believe her?
Mollie: Yes, I (8) _____ .
Jane: Really?

5 Write questions about a mystery person.

1 play / soccer / the mystery person?
Does the mystery person play soccer?
2 Where / live / the mystery person?
_____
3 What / do / the mystery person?
_____
4 you / know / the mystery person?
_____

SPEAK

6 Work in pairs.

- **Student A: look at page 115. Student B: look at page 116. Choose one of the people. Don't tell your partner.**
- **Ask and answer the questions in Exercise 5.**
- **Can you guess the name of your partner's mystery person?**

Is the mystery person a man or a woman?

She's a woman. / He's a man.

>>> **Listen to a radio show**

WORK WITH WORDS Daily activities

1 a **Work in pairs. Match the daily routine activities to the pictures.**

do my homework _____   finish school _____   go home _____   go to bed _____
go to school _____   get up _____   have breakfast _____   have dinner _____
have lunch _____   take a shower _____

b ▶2.24 **Listen and check. Then listen and repeat.**

2 **Put the activities in Exercise 1 in order for your day. Then compare with a partner.**

First I …   *Then I …*   *Next I …*

SPEAK AND LISTEN

3 **Work in pairs. Describe the pictures.**

1

4

2

5

3

PHRASE BYTES

In picture A the time's …
There's a …
I can see …

4 ▶2.25 **Listen to the radio show. What does Daniella's mom do? Where does she work?**

5 a ▶2.25 **Listen again. Read the questions and choose the correct picture (A, B, or C) from Exercise 3.**

1 What time does Daniella get up?   4 What does she do after school?
2 How does she go to school?   5 When does she go to bed?
3 What does she have for lunch?

b **Write five sentences about Daniella.**

She gets up at …

PHRASE BYTES

Daniella gets up at … I get up at …
School starts at …
My mom / dad goes to work at …

REACT

6 **Work in pairs. Ask and answer the questions.**
1 Is Daniella's daily routine the same as yours? What's different?
2 When does school start and finish in your country?
3 Does your mom or dad work? When does she/he work?

MOVE BEYOND

Do the Words & Beyond exercise on page 110.

GRAMMAR Adverbs of frequency

>>> **Say how often you do things**

READ >>> Grammar in context

1 **Read the survey and Holly's answers. What does she do in the evening?**

WHAT'S YOUR DAILY ROUTINE?
ANSWER THE QUESTIONS IN OUR SURVEY.

WHAT TIME DO YOU USUALLY GET UP?
My mom and dad are farmers, so I **often** get up at five to help them and give food to the animals.

HOW DO YOU GO TO SCHOOL?
I **usually** take the bus to school. My dad **sometimes** drives me.

HOW OFTEN DO YOU HAVE LUNCH AT SCHOOL?
I **always** have lunch at school. I can't go home.

AND WHAT DO YOU DO AFTER SCHOOL?
I **usually** go home and do my homework. My dad doesn't like TV, so I **never** watch it at home. I usually read a book. Then I go to bed at around nine o'clock.

STUDY

2 **Complete the line with the adverbs. Use Exercise 1 to help you.**

never   usually

```
100%                                         0%
|_____|_____|_____|_____|_____|
always            often      sometimes
```

3 **Complete the examples. Use Exercise 1 to help you.**

Adverbs of frequency
I _often_ get up at 5.
I _____ have lunch at school.
Questions
What time do you _____ get up?
How _____ do you have lunch at school?

See GRAMMAR DATABASE, page 102.

PRACTICE

4 **a** **Write the sentences with the adverbs of frequency in the correct place.**

1 I get up at at seven o'clock. (**usually**)
   I usually get up at seven o'clock.
2 I take a shower before breakfast. (**always**)

3 I take the bus to school. (**often**)

4 I read a book after dinner. (**sometimes**)

5 I go to bed before nine o'clock. (**never**)

b **Which of the sentences are true for you?**

>>> Workbook, page 62

5 **Write true sentences for you, your friends, and your family. Use adverbs of frequency.**

1 eat / chocolate
   My brother often eats chocolate.
2 go / to the movies
3 play / soccer on weekends
4 drink / coffee
5 take / the bus to school
6 watch / TV before school

6 **Circle the correct option.**

Marta: Hi, Simon! Do you (1)(*often*)/ *never* take the bus to school?
Simon: No, I don't. My mom (2) *never* / *usually* drives me on her way to work.
Marta: What does she do?
Simon: She's a teacher. She (3) *usually* / *never* starts work at 8:30, but she (4) *always* / *sometimes* starts at 7:30. How often do you take the bus?
Marta: I (5) *always* / *never* take the bus. I don't live near school, and my mom doesn't drive, so I (6) *never* / *sometimes* come by car.

7 **Do the survey.**

HOW OFTEN DO YOU DO THESE THINGS? CHECK (✓) THE CORRECT BOX.	0%	30%	60%	80%	100%
1 PLAY VIDEO GAMES					
2 GO SHOPPING					
3 GO ON THE INTERNET					
4 LISTEN TO MUSIC					
5 GET UP LATE					
6 READ A BOOK					

SPEAK

8 **Work in pairs. Ask and answer the questions in Exercise 7. Use adverbs of frequency.**

How often do you play video games?

I often play video games. And you?

I sometimes play them.

LANGUAGE &BEYOND

HELP! ✋ HOW OFTEN DO YOU NEED HELP TO ...

	OFTEN	SOMETIMES	NEVER
UNDERSTAND SOMETHING IN CLASS?			
DO HOMEWORK?			
FIND SOMETHING (CLOTHES, KEYS, ...)?			
USE SOMETHING (A COMPUTER, THE INTERNET, ...)?			

>>> **Ask for help**

SPEAK AND READ

1 Work in pairs. Describe the situation in the picture above.

2 Work in pairs. Look at the boy at the back on the left. Why doesn't he know the answer to the question? Check (✓) the possible answers.

_____ He doesn't have his paper.   _____ He doesn't understand the question.
_____ He's a new student.   _____ He can't hear the teacher.

> **PHRASE BYTES**
>
> It's a classroom.
> There's a ...
> There are some ...

DO

3 a Complete the HELP! survey above.

   b Who do you usually ask for help in the situations in the survey – your teacher, mom, dad, classmate, friend, brother, or sister? Why?

4 Work in pairs. Compare your answers to Exercise 3.

> *I often need help to do my homework.*

> *I sometimes need help. Who do you ask for help?*

> *I usually ask my big brother because ...*

5 Work in pairs. Match phrases 1–4 to the situations in the survey.
   1 "Mom? Can you help me with this exercise?"   3 "Can you repeat the question, please?"
   2 "Can you show me how to play this game?"   4 "I can't find my backpack. Can you help me find it?"

REFLECT

6 Talk about the questions. Then read the **REFLECTION POINT**.
   1 Why is it good to ask for help?
   2 Who do you ask for help in class and at home?
   3 What phrases can you use to ask for help?

> **PHRASE BYTES**
>
> It's good to ask for help because ...
> At home / In class I usually ask ...
> You can say ...

EXTEND

7 Work in pairs. Choose one of the situations in the survey and prepare a conversation. Then present it to other pairs.

> **REFLECTION POINT**
>
> It's important to ask for help if you don't understand something. In class, ask the teacher or other students. At home, ask your family.

SCHOOL SKILLS

>>>> Workbook, page 65

SPEAKING Why not?

>>> Ask for and give reasons

SPEAK

1  Work in pairs. Look at the picture and describe what you see.

PHRASE BYTES

She has …

Maybe he / she …

I think her father …

LISTEN

2 ▶2.26 Listen to the conversation. Why can't Annie do her homework?

Annie:	Dad? Are you busy?
Dad:	No. Why?
Annie:	Because (1) _____ .
Dad:	OK.
Annie:	Can I go and see Kate?
Dad:	No.
Annie:	Why not?
Dad:	Because (2) _____ .
Annie:	I can't do my homework.
Dad:	Why not?
Annie:	Because (3) _____ .
Dad:	Give it to me.
Annie:	Why?
Dad:	Because (4) _____ .
Annie:	OK. Here you are.
Dad:	Ah. I see why you need my help.
Annie:	Why?
Dad:	Because …

3 a Put the words in order to make phrases.

1 exercise / understand / don't / I / the _____
2 homework / have / you _____
3 help / I / you / can / maybe _____
4 you / I / question / ask / want / to / a _____

b Complete the conversation in Exercise 2 with the phrases.

4 ▶2.26 **Listen again and check your answers. Then complete the last line of the conversation in your own words.**

5 Match the questions to the reasons.

1 Why are you happy?
2 Why do you want to be a farmer?
3 Why isn't your sister here?
4 Why do we do homework?

a Because she's at the movies.
b Because we need to practice.
c Because I like animals.
d Because it's Saturday.

ACT

6  **Work in pairs. Complete the tasks.**

- Read the first lines of the conversations.
  "How do you usually go to school?"
  "Who's your favorite soccer player?"
  "Do you like classical music?"
  "Mom? Can I go to the movies?"
- Continue the conversations with *why* and *because*.
- Practice the conversations.
- Present one of your conversations to other students.

PHRASEBOOK ▶2.27

Ask for reasons

(*Give it to me.*)

Why?

(*I can't do my homework.*)

Why not?

Give reasons

Because I / you / it …

WRITING A normal day

SPEAK AND READ

1 **Work in pairs. Check (✓) the things you do on a school day. How often do you do them? Compare your answers with your partner.**

get up late		chat with friends
have a sandwich		watch TV
do homework		ride a bike

2 **Read the website post. Which of the things in Exercise 1 does Sally do?**

ASK ANY QUESTION

| Home | Technology | Health | Sports | History | World |

Q: What's a normal school day for kids in Australia?

In Australia we usually get up at seven o'clock and have breakfast. School starts at nine o'clock. We have lunch at one o'clock, but we don't have free school meals in Australia. I often have a sandwich. I finish school at three o'clock. Then I go home and do my homework. I usually go to bed at nine o'clock, but I sometimes watch television until 9:30.

Sally G., Mount Gambier, Australia

3 **Read the tips in the `HOW TO` box. Then <u>underline</u> examples of *and* and *but* in the website post.**

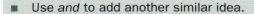

HOW TO

use *and* and *but*

- Use *and* to add another similar idea.
- Use *but* to add a different idea.

PRACTICE

4 **Use *and* or *but* to join the sentences. Use a comma before *and* and *but*.**

1 I like ice cream. I don't like chocolate ice cream.
I like ice cream, but I don't like chocolate ice cream.

2 My sister doesn't play an instrument. She loves music.

3 There's a clock on the wall. There are some pictures.

4 On Sundays we usually go to the movies. We have dinner at a restaurant.

5 I usually go to bed at nine. On Saturdays I go to bed at 10.

6 They don't have free school meals in Australia. They have free school meals in some countries.

DISCUSS

5 **Talk about a normal school day in your country. What time does school start and end? When and where do you have lunch? Are these things true for all students in your country?**

WRITE

6 **Write a website post about a normal school day in your country.**

1 Write about a school day in your country. Answer these questions: When does school start? What do students usually eat for lunch? Do they get lunch at school? What time does school end? What do students usually do after school?

2 Use adverbs of frequency. Write about how often you do things using *always*, *usually*, *sometimes*, *never*.

3 Connect short sentences with *and* and *but*. See the `HOW TO` box.

SHARE

7 **Take turns reading your website posts. What's different? What's the same?**

VOCABULARY Jobs

1 Write the jobs.

MEET YOUR ME2! YOUR ME2 CAN ...

1 work in a store. _____
2 help students learn things. _____
3 take people's food to their restaurant table.
   _____
4 work in a theater. _____
5 make food in a restaurant. _____
6 help people in a hospital. _____
7 help the doctor at the hospital. _____
8 work with animals. _____
9 play soccer. _____
10 welcome people to a hotel. _____

___ /10

Daily activities

2 Complete the daily routine phrases with the verbs in the box.

> does   finishes   gets   goes (x2)   has (x3)
> take   walk

FOLLOW THE DAILY ROUTINE OF YOUR ME2!

Me2 (1) _____ up at five o'clock every day.
It (2) _____ a shower, and then it
(3) _____ breakfast. Me2 (4) _____
to school. It (5) _____ lunch at school
(a special Me2 sandwich). Me2 (6) _____ school
at 3:30. After school it (7) _____ home and
(8) _____ its homework. It (9) _____ dinner
at 7:30 and (10) _____ to bed at 9:00.

___ /10

GRAMMAR Simple present

3 Choose the correct options to complete the conversation.

ME2   HOME   FAQ   ABOUT

Q: (1) *Do / Does* I need the internet to use Me2?
A: Yes, you (2) *do / don't* . First you register on the website. Then you choose a name and a job for your Me2.
Q: (3) *Do / Does* other people see my personal information?
A: No, they (4) *don't / doesn't* . They only see your Me2 information.
Q: How much (5) *do / does* it cost?
A: It (6) *don't / doesn't* cost anything. It's free!
Q: (7) *Do / Does* Me2 sleep?
A: Yes, it (8) *do / does* .

___ /16

Adverbs of frequency

4 Rewrite the sentences. Write an adverb of frequency from the box in the correct place in each sentence.

> always (x2)   never (x2)   often
> sometimes   usually

1 How do you visit the Me2 website?
2 I visit it in the morning after breakfast. (100%)
3 I visit the website at school because my teacher doesn't like it. (0%)
4 Me2 wants to talk to me. (100%)
5 We talk about soccer. (80%)
6 We play video games. (30%)
7 But I win! (0%)

___ /14

Your score: ___ /50

SKILLS CHECK

✓✓✓	Yes, I can. No problem!
✓✓	Yes, I can. But I need a little help.
✓	Yes, I can. But I need a lot of help.

I can read a questionnaire. _____
I can listen to a radio show. _____
I can ask for help. _____
I can ask for and give reasons. _____
I can write a website post. _____

6 UNIT

VACATION HOME

TOP TENTS

IN THE PICTURE Our vacation home »»

>>> **Talk about homes**

WORK WITH WORDS Homes

1 **RECALL** Work in pairs. Complete the things in a room with *a, e, i, o,* and *u*. You have two minutes.

1 b___d
2 ch_____r
3 cl___ck
4 c___mp___t___r

5 d____sk
6 d____r
7 fl_____r
8 l____ght

9 p____ct_____r
10 t___bl_
11 w____ll
12 w_____ndow

2 a ▶2.28 **Listen. Where does Oscar live? Choose the correct place.**

a

an apartment with swimming pool

b

an apartment with big balcony

c

a house with yard and terrace

b ▶2.29 **Listen and repeat the words.**

3 🔊 **Look at the plan and the pictures of Oscar's vacation home. What sort of vacation home is it? How many rooms does it have?**

4 a ▶2.30 **Listen. Write the correct words from the box for 1–7 on the plan.**

> bathroom   bedroom (x2)   dining room   hall   living room   kitchen

b ▶2.31 **Listen and check. Then listen and repeat.**

5 **Write the correct words from Exercises 2 and 4.**

1 You eat in this room. _____
2 You sleep in this room. _____
3 You swim here. _____
4 You take a shower here. _____
5 You cook in this room. _____

6 You sit outside here. _____ / _____ / _____
7 You sit or watch TV or talk in this room. _____
8 You come in or go to other rooms here. _____
9 You live here in a big city. _____
10 This has many rooms and a yard. _____

PHRASE BYTES

It's an apartment / a hotel / a tent / a house.

It has …

Luxury Camping In
Beautiful Tents

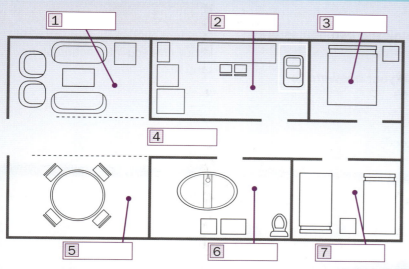

6 **THE MOVING PICTURE** ▶ **Watch the video. What does Oscar do on vacation?**

SPEAK

7 a Draw a plan of your home. Don't write the names of the rooms.

b Work in pairs. Ask and answer about your homes.

I live in a house / an apartment.

What room's that?

That's the living room / my parents' bedroom / my room.

Do you have a balcony / yard / swimming pool?

Yes, we do. / No, we don't.

MOVE BEYOND

Do the Words & Beyond exercise on page 111.

READING Home away from home

READ

1 Look at the pictures. Where do you think the two homes are? What are the places like?

2 ▶2.32 Read the chat messages. Check your answers to Exercise 1 and complete the sentences.

1 Josina usually lives in _____ .
2 Ricardo usually lives in _____ .
3 Now, Josina is in _____ and Ricardo is in _____ because they're on a house _____ .

READING TIP

Look at pictures before you read. They give you information about the text.

MOVE BEYOND   INSTANT MESSENGER   PROFILES SETTINGS FRIENDS

JOSINA   RICARDO

JOSINA: Hi, Ricardo. Is everything OK there? We're in your home! I love it! I love your room. Your bed's more comfortable than mine!

RICARDO: I love your houseboat! Your home is really cool.

JOSINA: Is it your first time in Europe?

RICARDO: Yes, it is. I like the Netherlands. It's quieter than at home. And it's very clean.

JOSINA: It's my first time in Latin America too. Mexico City is much bigger and noisier than Amsterdam. It's exciting here!

RICARDO: Do you like the view from the apartment?

JOSINA: Yes, it's fantastic. All those tall buildings!

RICARDO: A house exchange is a great idea. It's more interesting than a boring, expensive hotel. I don't like hotels.

JOSINA: Really? I love hotels. My parents are terrible cooks. Hotel food is better than their cooking. Oh … it's one thirty – nearly time for lunch.

RICARDO: That's right. It's seven hours later in Amsterdam. It's time for dinner here.

😊 ⌄   ABC ⌄

YOUR MESSAGE | SEND

3 Read the messages again. Choose the correct answer (A, B, or C).

1 Josina …
   A thinks Ricardo's home is OK.   B doesn't think his bed is comfortable.
   C likes Ricardo's room.
2 This is Ricardo's …
   A first visit to Latin America.   B first visit to Europe.   C first time on a boat.
3 The apartment in Mexico City …
   A has a great view.   B is very quiet.   C is like a hotel.
4 Ricardo thinks a house exchange is …
   A OK.   B interesting.   C a bad idea.
5 Josina likes hotels because her parents …
   A always stay in hotels.   B make great food.   C can't cook.
6 In Amsterdam the time is …
   A 8:30 p.m.   B 1:30 p.m.   C 11:30 p.m.

PHRASE BYTES

We go to …

My favorite house exchange home is a / an …

A … is better than … because …

REACT

4 🔊 Work in pairs. What do you think? Tell your partner.

1 Your parents want to do a house exchange. Where do you go?
2 What kind of home do you choose for your exchange?
3 Is a house exchange better than a hotel? Why or why not?

MOVE BEYOND

Underline all the adjectives (OK, comfortable, …) in the text.

 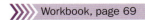

GRAMMAR Comparative adjectives

>>> Compare two places, people, or things

READ AND LISTEN >>> Grammar in context

1 ▶2.33 **Read and listen to the conversation. Which city is more popular – New York or Washington? Why?**

Grace: What's the capital city of the USA?
Lola: New York.
Grace: No! It's Washington, DC. A lot of people think New York's the capital because it's bigger and more famous than Washington. Washington is smaller and quieter, but maybe it's more dangerous.
Lola: Oh. But New York is cooler! It's in a lot of American movies.
Grace: This website says New York is dirtier and more expensive than Washington. But New York is more popular because the stores and restaurants are better.

STUDY

2 **Complete the examples. Use Exercise 1 to help you.**

Comparative adjectives
One-syllable adjective + -er
small > _smaller_   cool > _____
Washington is _____ and quieter.
SPELLING: big > _bigger_   dirty > _dirtier_
more + adjectives with two or more syllables
famous > _more famous_
dangerous > _____
New York is _____ popular.
Irregular adjectives
good > _better_   bad > _worse_
far > _further/farther_
New York restaurants are _____ .

See GRAMMAR DATABASE, page 103.

3 **Complete the sentences with the correct word.**
1 New York's bigger _____ Washington.
2 New York's dirtier _____ Washington.

PRACTICE

4 **Complete the sentences with the correct form of the comparative.**
1 **Peru:** Lima is _bigger_ (**big**) than Arequipa.
2 **Italy:** Rome is _____ (**far**) from the beach than Venice.
3 **Canada:** Toronto is _____ (**expensive**) than Ottawa.
4 **Venezuela:** Caracas is _____ (**interesting**) than Valencia.
5 **The USA:** San Antonio is _____ (**cheap**) than New York.
6 **Brazil:** Rio is _____ (**old**) than Brasilia.

5 a **Compare the two vacation places. Write six sentences with the adjectives.**

1 _Wonderville is safer than Superville._

b **Compare two towns or places in your country. Write three to five sentences.**

SPEAK

6 **Work in pairs. Student A: look at page 115. Student B: look at page 116.**
Find out which trip is:
– longer
– more expensive
– more comfortable
– more interesting

My trip is for … days.

My trip is for … . Mine's shorter/longer.

I think my/your trip's more interesting because …

LISTENING AND VOCABULARY Favorite food

>>> **Understand a conversation about food**

WORK WITH WORDS Food and drink

1 a Work in pairs. What food and drinks can you remember from Units 1–5? Make a list.

b Answer the questions about your list.

1 Which things are food?
2 Which things are drinks?
3 Which things are fruit?

2 a ▶2.34 Look at more food and drinks. Listen to Corey. Match the words to the pictures.

bread	cheese	chicken	egg
juice	meat	milk	oil
pasta	rice	steak	vegetables

b ▶2.35 Listen and check. Then listen and repeat.

3 🗣 Work in pairs. Tell your partner:
- what food and drinks you like and don't like.
- how often you eat or drink them.
- when you eat or drink them.

LISTEN

4 a ▶2.36 Read the note for Corey's family and listen. What food do they have in the house? Check (✓) the food in Exercise 2a.

b ▶2.36 Listen again. Match the people (1–5) to the food they like (a–h).

1	Corey	a	chicken
2	mom	b	pizza
3	dad	c	milk
4	sister	d	pasta
5	brother	e	juice
		f	steak
		g	vegetables
		h	cheese

REACT

5 🗣 Work in pairs. Ask and answer.

1 What's your favorite food?
2 What food is popular in your country?
3 Do you like food from other countries? What food?

PHRASE BYTES

I like / don't like …

I sometimes / never / often eat …

I eat … for breakfast / lunch / dinner / after school.

HELLO, JOHNSON FAMILY. WELCOME TO ITALY! THERE'S SOME FOOD FOR YOU IN THE REFRIGERATOR AND IN THE CABINET. ENJOY YOUR VACATION!

THE BERTOLINO FAMILY

PHRASE BYTES

My favorite food is …

Rice / pasta is popular in my country.

I like Chinese / Italian / Mexican food.

MOVE BEYOND

Do the Words & Beyond exercise on page 111.

>>> Workbook, pages 72–73

READ AND LISTEN >>> Grammar in context

1 ▶2.37 **Read and listen. Which fact in Dad's book is most interesting?**

Dad: I have some great facts about Italian food. How many courses are there in a meal? Do you have any ideas?

Corey: Three?

Dad: Four. First there are some vegetables, then there's some pasta. Then there's some meat or fish – but Italians don't eat much meat – and then something sweet. Pasta cooks fast. How many minutes do you cook pasta?

Mom: Ten.

Dad: No, five to six. How much pasta does an Italian eat in a year? More than 27 kilos!

Corey: Wow, that's a lot of pasta! How much ice cream do Italians eat?

Dad: Sorry, the book doesn't have any facts about that.

STUDY

2 **Complete the table with the words in the box. Use Exercise 1 to help you. Use plural nouns when you need them.**

course	fish	ice cream	minute

Countable	Uncountable
a fact, some facts	pasta, some pasta
a _____, some	_____, some
a _____, some	_____, some

See GRAMMAR DATABASE, page 103.

3 **Complete with examples from Exercise 1.**

Many (countable)	Much (uncountable)
How many _courses_ are there in a meal?	How much _____ does an Italian eat in a year?
How many _____ do you cook pasta?	Italians don't eat much _____.

Some (count/uncountable)	Any (count/uncountable)
I have _____ great facts about Italian food.	Do you have _any_ pasta?
There's some _____.	The book doesn't have _____ facts about that.

See GRAMMAR DATABASE, page 103.

4 a ▶2.38 **PRONOUNCE** **Listen and repeat the /ʌ/ sound in m*u*ch and s*o*me.**

b ▶2.39 **Listen and repeat these words.**

br*o*ther   c*ou*ntry   d*oe*s   h*u*ndred   l*o*ve

PRACTICE

5 a **After a shopping trip, the Johnson family has a lot of food. Complete the sentences with *some* or *any*.**

1 There's _some_ meat.
2 There aren't _____ bananas.
3 There's _____ milk.
4 There are _____ burgers.
5 There aren't _____ oranges.
6 There isn't _____ fruit salad.

b **Complete the conversation.**

Corey: Mom, are there (1) _any_ apples?
Mom: No, there (2) _____.
Corey: Is there (3) _____ melon?
Mom: No, there (4) _____.
Corey: Is there (5) _____ juice?
Mom: Yes, there (6) _____.

6 a **Write questions with *much* or *many*.**

1 How / eggs / there?
   How many eggs are there?
2 How / cheese / there?
3 How / vegetables / there?
4 How / burgers / there?
5 How / chicken / there?
6 How / bottles of water / there?

b **Work in pairs. Look at the refrigerator in Exercise 5. Ask and answer.**

> How much/many … ?

> There isn't much / aren't many.

> There's / There are a lot of …

SPEAK

7 a **Work in pairs. Student A: look at your cabinet on page 115. Say what's in it. Student B: draw the cabinet.**

b **Student B: look at your freezer on page 116. Say what's in it. Student A: draw the freezer.**

LANGUAGE &BEYOND

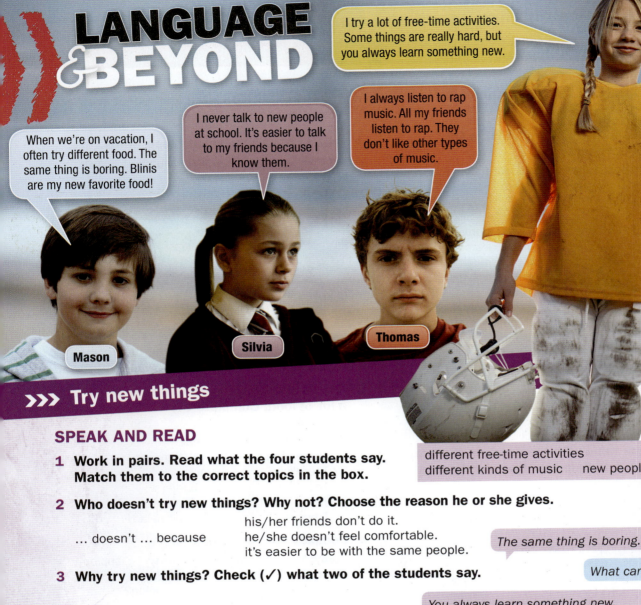

> I try a lot of free-time activities. Some things are really hard, but you always learn something new.

Catalina

> When we're on vacation, I often try different food. The same thing is boring. Blinis are my new favorite food!

Mason

> I never talk to new people at school. It's easier to talk to my friends because I know them.

Silvia

> I always listen to rap music. All my friends listen to rap. They don't like other types of music.

Thomas

>>> Try new things

SPEAK AND READ

1 **Work in pairs. Read what the four students say. Match them to the correct topics in the box.**

> different free-time activities
> different kinds of music   new people   new food

2 **Who doesn't try new things? Why not? Choose the reason he or she gives.**

... doesn't ... because
- his/her friends don't do it.
- he/she doesn't feel comfortable.
- it's easier to be with the same people.

> The same thing is boring. _____

3 **Why try new things? Check (✓) what two of the students say.**

> What can you lose? _____

DO

> You always learn something new. _____

> It's fun! _____

4 **Make the sentences true for you. Write *often*, *sometimes*, or *never*.**

1 I try different food. _____
2 I listen to different kinds of music. _____
3 I try different free-time activities. _____
4 I make new friends and talk to different people. _____
5 I watch different kinds of TV programs and movies. _____

5 **Work in pairs. Read your sentences to your partner. Ask why or why not.**

> I never try different food.   Why not?   Because sometimes I don't like it.

REFLECT

6  **Talk about the questions. Then read the** **REFLECTION POINT**.

1 Do you often try new things?
2 Why don't you try new things?
3 Why is it good to try new things?

EXTEND

7 **Work in pairs. Decide what new things you can try.**

> I always eat cheese sandwiches for lunch. I can try a salad.

> I play soccer. I can try basketball.

PHRASE BYTES

I often try new food.

I don't try new things because ...

REFLECTION POINT ««

It's easier (but sometimes boring) to do the same things. Try new things! You can learn something new, make new friends, and have more fun!

SCHOOL SKILLS

SPEAK

1 Work in pairs. What do people often buy when they're on vacation? Look at the pictures and make a list together.

People often buy vacation souvenirs like …

Vacation souvenirs

Food and drink

Clothes

LISTEN

2 ▶2.40 Listen to the conversations. What thing in Exercise 1 does each person ask about? How much is it? Complete the conversations.

1
Joel: Hi. How much is this (1) _____ ?
Clerk: It's (2) _____ dollars.
Joel: OK. Can I have some, please?

2
April: Hello. How much is this (3) _____ ?
Clerk: It's (4) _____ dollars.
April: Sorry, that's too much.

3
Megan: How much are these (5) _____ ,
           please?
Clerk: They're (6) _____ dollars.
Megan: OK. Can I have them, please?

4
Mark: Hi. How much are the (7) _____ ?
Clerk: They're (8) _____ dollar.
Mark: Mmm. I'm not sure. Thanks.

3 **a** ▶2.41 Look at the questions in the conversations. Listen and repeat.

   b Make questions.

How much is
- these bags?
- that fruit salad?
- the soccer shirt?

How much are
- those pens?
- the sunglasses?
- this ice cream?

4 **a** ▶2.40 Listen to conversations 1–4 again. Who buys the thing? Who doesn't buy the thing?

Joel/April/Megan/Mark buys …
… doesn't buy …

   b ▶2.42 Listen and repeat the sentences.

ACT

5   Work in pairs. You are in the market in Exercise 1. Practice two conversations.
Student A: ask how much something is.
Student B: say a price.
Student A: buy or don't buy the thing.
Change roles. Then practice two more conversations.

PHRASEBOOK ▶2.43

Ask how much something is

How much is the orange juice / this T-shirt / that … ?

How much are the notebooks / these … / those … ?

Buy or not buy something

OK. Can I have some / it / them, please?

Sorry, that's too much.

I'm not sure. Thanks.

WRITING Back home

⟫⟫⟫ Write a text message

READ

1 **Look at the picture. What's this food? Where do people eat it?**

2 **Read the text message. Who's it to? What's it about?**

9:30 am

Hi Jake, we're back from vacation! It's colder here than in Alicante. It's grayer too. ☹ I miss the beach and the food. There aren't many bad things about Alicante! There are some good stores, and I have some great souvenirs. I have a present for you too. See you tomorrow at school!

3 **Read the tips in the HOW TO box. Then <u>underline</u> two sentences with *too* in the text message.**

HOW TO	❓

use *too*

- Use *too* to add another similar idea.
- Use *too* at the end of a sentence.

PRACTICE

4 **Add a similar idea. Use *too*.**

1 I like vegetables.
   I like vegetables. I like fruit too.
2 I often listen to music.
3 I have a cat.
4 There are two bedrooms in our apartment.
5 I get up late on Saturdays.
6 I can speak English.

DISCUSS

5 **Think about your last vacation. Talk about how that place is different from your home.**

   Is it more interesting or more boring? Is it colder or hotter?

WRITE

6 **Write a text message to a friend after your vacation.**

1 Say you are back. Compare your home to your vacation place. What good things are in that place? Do you miss the food or activities in that place?
2 Use comparative adjectives to describe how the vacation place is different from home.
3 Use *too* to add more ideas. See the **HOW TO** box.

SHARE

7 **Exchange your text messages with other students and read them. Decide which vacation place you like best.**

VOCABULARY Homes

1 **Complete the website post with the words in the box.**

> apartment   balcony   bathroom   bedroom
> dining room   hall   house   kitchen   living room
> terrace   swimming pool   yard

myvacationplace.net

Tell us about your vacation places and activities!

Luis, USA

Our vacation home in Mexico isn't a small (1) _____ –
it's a big (2) _____ . It has a (3) _____ outside
with trees and a big blue (4) _____ in it. There's also a
nice (5) _____ where we can eat meals outside. There's
a big (6) _____ on the second floor. Mom and Dad often
sit outside there. There's a small (7) _____ when you
come in. There are three (8) _____ s to sleep in. Each
one has a (9) _____ . There's a big (10) _____ to
cook food and a (11) _____ to eat meals, and there's a
(12) _____ with a big TV. I want to stay here!

___ /12

Food and drink

2 **Complete the words.**

Bobby, USA

Spain is a great vacation place. The
food at the hotel is fantastic! They
have all my favorite things:
- (1) br _____ d (you eat it with
  (2) o _____)
- (3) ch _____ e
- (4) ch _____ en
- (5) e _____ s
- a lot of fish but not much
  (6) m _____ t like
  (7) s _____ k
- orange (8) j _____ ce
- (9) r _____ e (mm … , paella!)
- (10) a lot of
  ve _____ es
(But there isn't much
(11) p _____ a, and you can't
get tea with (12) m _____ k.)

___ /12

GRAMMAR Comparative adjectives

3 **Complete the opinions with comparative adjectives.**

What do you think?

① Math homework is _____ (**easy**)
than English homework!

② A tent is _____ (**nice**)
than a house!

③ Shopping with my friends is _____
(**boring**) than playing video games.

④ T-shirts are _____
(**comfortable**) than my school uniform.

⑤ Hotel food is _____ (**good**)
than school lunches.

⑥ I like animals! For me, horses are
_____ (**interesting**) than dogs!

___ /12

Some and any, much and many

4 **Choose the correct options to complete the questions and answers.**

Vacation Q & A

Q How (1) *much* / *many* water do you need to
drink when it's very warm?

A A lot! Always carry (2) *some* / *any* water with
you.

Q How (3) *much* / *many* money do I need for two
days in Belize?

A Belize isn't expensive. You don't need
(4) *much* / *many* money.

Q I don't like rice. How (5) *much* / *many* rice do
people eat in Italy?

A They don't usually eat (6) *some* / *any* rice. There
aren't (7) *much* / *many* things with rice.

___ /14

Your score: ___ /50

SKILLS CHECK

✓✓✓	Yes, I can. No problem!
✓✓	Yes, I can. But I need a little help.
✓	Yes, I can. But I need a lot of help.

I can read chat messages. _____
I can understand a conversation about food. _____
I can try new things. _____
I can ask how much something is. _____
I can write a text message. _____

⟫⟫⟫ **Workbook, pages 78–79**

READ

1 Match the sentences (1–5) to the correct signs (A–H).

Example:

0	Fruit isn't expensive here.	*D*
1	You can buy this apartment.	....
2	Small kids can't swim here.	....
3	You can have breakfast, lunch, and dinner here.	....
4	You can get help in the hotel here.	....
5	You can eat this for school lunch.	....

A

Cozy Café

Open from 6 a.m. to 10 p.m.

B

Do you need information?
Please ask the receptionist.
→

C

POOL OPEN FROM
10 UNTIL 6 EVERY DAY

D

CHEAP GRAPES,
BANANAS, AND
WATERMELON

E

Ask your waiter about this week's
SPECIAL MEALS

F

FOR SALE
Three-room apartment
with kitchen and
bathroom

G

STUDENTS' MENU
- CHICKEN AND PASTA
- FRUIT SALAD
- ORANGE JUICE OR WATER

H

NO CHILDREN
UNDER 6 YEARS OLD IN
THE POOL.

Reading: _____ /10

LISTEN

2 **2.44 Listen to Matt talking to Emma about his mom's and dad's jobs. For each question, choose the correct answer (A, B, or C).**

Example:

0   What does Matt's mom do?
   A   She's a doctor.
   B   She's an actor.
   C   She's a cook.

1   When does Matt watch his mom?
   A   sometimes
   B   often
   C   never

2   Matt's dad has a …
   A   store.
   B   restaurant.
   C   café.

3   Matt's dad works from …
   A   7 a.m. to 7 p.m.
   B   7 a.m. to 10 p.m.
   C   7 a.m. to 11 p.m.

4   Matt's dad's job is …
   A   fantastic.
   B   hard.
   C   exciting.

5   Matt's mom …
   A   works every night.
   B   works nearly every night.
   C   doesn't work every night.

Listening: _____ /10

WRITE

3   Read Jordan's invitation and message to Sam. Then complete Sam's notes.

Jordan's Picnic

Come to my big birthday picnic in City Park – Sunday the 11th at 12:00.
We have a lot of food, and after the picnic we can play some games too.
Hope you can come – call me by Friday at 873-4193.

Sam, thanks for the offer to come earlier and help with everything. We can make the food at home, but we need some help at the park before the picnic. Can you come at 11:15? Bring your soccer ball, and don't forget to wear your new soccer shirt too! 😊 😊

Jordan's picnic

Why?   _birthday_
Place: (1) _____
Day and date: (2) _____
Come at: (3) _____
Take: (4) _____
Remember: your (5) _____

Writing: _____ / 10

Progress check score _____ /30

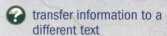

THEATER WORKSHOP

IN THE PICTURE What are you wearing?

>>> Talk about clothes

WORK WITH WORDS Clothes

1 a **RECALL** Work in pairs. Write the names of the colors. You have one minute.

1 red

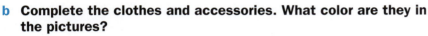

b **Complete the clothes and accessories. What color are they in the pictures?**

1 j _____ s _____
2 s _____ t _____
3 b ___ g _____
4 s _____ g _____ s _____

2 ▶2.45 Listen to the descriptions. Match them to the pictures.

3 a **Match the clothes (1–10) in the pictures to the words in the box.**

dress	hat	jacket	pants	shirt
shoes	skirt	sneakers	socks	sweatshirt

b ▶2.46 **Listen and check. Then listen and repeat.**

4 a ▶2.47 **PRONOUNCE** Listen and repeat the /s/ sound in these words.

<u>s</u>chool <u>s</u>it <u>s</u>on <u>s</u>treet <u>s</u>unglasses

b ▶2.48 **In Exercise 3a, <u>underline</u> four more words with the /s/ sound at the beginning. Then listen and repeat.**

5 ▶2.49 **Look at the pictures again. Complete the sentences with words from Exercise 3a. Then listen and check.**

1 So you're wearing blue _____, white _____, and a red _____ .
2 I like the big _____ . Very nice.
3 I'm wearing a green _____ and a brown shirt.
4 We have a black _____ , a pink _____ , and some jeans. Are those orange _____ ? Let's see. Wow!
5 Yeah. It looks good. The yellow bag with the purple _____ , and the brown _____ are good. I like it.

6 **THE MOVING PICTURE** ▶ **Watch the video. What are these students wearing? Describe their clothes.**

SPEAK

7 Work in pairs. Ask and answer the questions.

1 What clothes do you usually wear at school?
2 What do you wear at home?
3 What do you wear when you go out?

I usually wear …

At school/home I wear …

When I go out, I …

MOVE BEYOND

Do the Words & Beyond exercise on page 112.

>>> **Read part of a play**

SPEAK AND READ

1 Work in pairs. Ask and answer the questions.

1 How often do you go to the theater or movies?
2 Who are your favorite actors?
3 Are you a good actor?

2 ▶2.50 Read the play and write the names of the people in the pictures.

a Queen

SCENE ONE:

The hall of King Harold's castle. There's a table with two chairs in the hall. GUARD 1 is sitting on one of the chairs. GUARD 2 is drinking some water. ALEX runs into the hall. ALEX is wearing a hat, a jacket, and pants. GUARD 1 stands up.

Guard 1: Who's there?
Alex: A friend! Where are the king and queen?
Guard 2: They're eating. What do you want, boy?
Alex: I have a message – some important news. The Black Prince is coming.
Guard 1: I don't believe you. Stop him!

The GUARDS stop ALEX.

Alex: Let me go!

The KING and QUEEN walk into the hall.

King: What's happening here?
Guard 1: It's this boy, sir.
Alex: I'm not a boy. I'm a girl!
Guard 2: You're wearing a boy's clothes.
King: Speak, boy … girl! Why are you here?
Alex: It's the Black Prince. He's bringing 100 men here.
King: What are you saying?
Queen: She's saying the Black Prince – our son – wants to be king.
King: Where are they now?
Alex: Right now they're sleeping in tents on the other side of town.
Queen: Then we have a problem!

3 Read the descriptions and write the words from the play.

1 Kings and queens often live here. _____ (6 letters)
2 This person keeps other people safe. _____ (5 letters)
3 Information that you give or send to someone. _____ (7 letters)
4 The son of a king and queen. _____ (6 letters)
5 Another way to say "now." _____ (2 words, 5 and 3 letters)
6 A difficult situation. _____ (7 letters)

4 ▶2.50 Complete the tasks.

1 Form a group with four other students.
2 Each student chooses a different person from the play.
3 Listen to the play again. Then read the play. Each student says his or her person's lines.

REACT

5 🗣 Work in pairs. What do you think? Tell your partner.

1 What does the Black Prince want to do?
2 What clothes does Alex wear in the scene? Why?
3 What happens next?

>>> Workbook, page 81

>>> Talk about things happening now

READ >>> Grammar in context

1 Read Bella's text message. What is Veronique wearing?

Hello from Ottawa, the capital of Canada. I'm sending you a picture of my classmates. We aren't studying today. We're taking a day off. Right now we're walking and shopping downtown. (I'm not shopping because I don't have any money!) That's Claude with Eric. He's wearing the sweatshirt with the blue stripes. He usually wears sunglasses, but he isn't wearing sunglasses now. Veronique is walking next to him. She's wearing white pants.

STUDY

2 Complete the examples. Use Exercise 1 to help you.

Present progressive
Affirmative
Use the verb *be* + base verb + *-ing*.
I _____ sending you a picture.
He _____ the sweatshirt.
We're walking and _____ .
Negative
Use the verb *be* + not + verb + *-ing*.
I'm not shopping .
He isn't wearing sunglasses now.
We _____ today.
Spelling
send > _____
take > _____
sho**p** > _____
Time Expressions
now
_____ now
today
at the moment

See GRAMMAR DATABASE, page 104.

>>> Workbook, pages 82–83

PRACTICE

3 Write the *-ing* form of the verbs.

1 make _making_   4 play _____
2 read _____   5 sit _____
3 ride _____   6 sleep _____

4 Write sentences in the present progressive.

1 I / wear / a pink shirt.
  I'm wearing a pink shirt.
2 We / watch / a video.
  _____
3 Our teacher / write / on the board.
  _____
4 Students / sing / in the next room.
  _____
5 My best friend / swim.
  _____
6 My mom and dad / drive / to work.
  _____

5 Make the sentences in Exercise 4 true for you. Use the present progressive affirmative and negative.

At the moment …
1 _I'm not wearing a pink shirt. I'm wearing a white shirt._

6 Complete the message with the present progressive.

Hello again from Ottawa!
We (1) _'re having_ (have) a fantastic time. I (2) _____ (write) this postcard on the bus. We (3) _____ (take) it to the Science and Technology Museum. The other students (4) _____ (sing). Veronique (5) _____ (sit) next to me. She (6) _____ (listen) to music.

SPEAK

7 Work in pairs. Student A: look at page 115. Student B: look at page 116.

- Describe your picture to your partner.
- Find six differences. Don't look at your partner's picture.

In my picture there's a girl. She's wearing a red skirt.

In my picture she's wearing a blue skirt.

LISTENING AND VOCABULARY Mime show

>>> Listen to descriptions

SPEAK AND LISTEN

1 Work in pairs. Choose an action and mime it (act without words). Can your partner guess the action?

eat   listen   read   talk on the phone   sleep

2 ▶2.51 Listen and match the conversations to the pictures.

1 _____   2 _____   3 _____   4 _____   5 _____

a

b

c

d

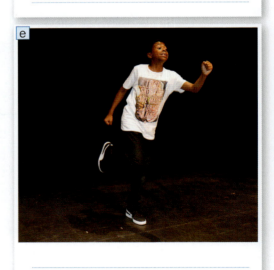
e

3 ▶2.52 Listen and check your answers.

WORK WITH WORDS Action verbs

4 a Write the verbs from the conversations under the pictures.

carry   dance   drive   fly   point   run
shop   sit   stand   swim   talk   wait

b ▶2.53 Listen and check. Then listen and repeat.

5 a Complete the sentences about the mime show with the verbs in Exercise 4a. Use the present progressive.

1 She *'s standing* _____ in the street. She _____ for someone.
2 He _____ a bag. He _____ at something. He _____ .
3 They _____ in a car. She _____ , and he _____ on the phone.
4 He _____ . No, he isn't. He _____ !
5 He _____ in a pool. No, he _____ .

b ▶2.54 Listen and check.

REACT

6 Work in pairs. Complete the tasks.

1 Describe the mime scene you like best. Can your partner point to the correct picture?
2 Mime a new scene. Can your partner say what's happening?

> You're sitting at a table.

> You're eating.

MOVE BEYOND

Do the Words & Beyond exercise on page 112.

GRAMMAR Present progressive

>>> **Ask and answer questions about things happening now**

READ AND LISTEN >>> Grammar in context

1 ▶2.55 **Read and listen to the conversation. When is Sally's party?**

Patrick: Hi, Sally. What's happening?
Sally: Nothing.
Patrick: Oh. Where are the others? Are they waiting in the living room?
Sally: No, they aren't. Jake and David are shopping.
Patrick: Is Melanie making a cake?
Sally: No, she isn't.
Patrick: Oh.
Sally: What are you doing here? Why are you wearing that costume?
Patrick: You're having a costume party today. Remember? Are you having a costume party today, Sally?
Sally: No, I'm not. The party's *next* Saturday. Patrick? Where are you going?

STUDY

2 **Complete the examples. Use Exercise 1 to help you.**

Present progressive
Questions
Are you having a costume party?
Are they _____ in the living room?
_____ Melanie _____ a cake?
What _____ are you doing here?
_____ you _____ that costume?
_____ are you going?
Short answers
Yes, I am. / *No, I'm not* .
Yes, she is. / No, she _____ .
Yes, they are. / No, _____ .

See **GRAMMAR DATABASE**, page 104.

PRACTICE

3 **Complete the sentences with the correct form of *be*.**

1 Hi, Patrick. What ___*are*___ you doing?
2 _____ I calling the right number?
3 _____ Patrick sleeping?
4 What _____ he doing?
5 _____ they shopping at the mall?
6 Why _____ you using Patrick's phone?

4 a **Match the answers to the questions in Exercise 3.**

a He's shopping with some friends. _____
b Because mine isn't working. _____
c No, he isn't. _____
d I'm not Patrick. I'm his brother. ___1___
e Yes, they are. _____
f Yes, you are. _____

b ▶2.56 **Listen and check your answers to Exercises 3 and 4a.**

5 **Write questions in the present progressive.**

1 What / the teacher / do / right now?
   What's the teacher doing right now?
2 Who / sit / next to you?

3 you / feel / happy right now?

4 What / the teacher / wear / today?

5 we / study / the simple present / now?

6 What / you / think / about?

SPEAK

6 **Work in pairs. Ask and answer the questions in Exercise 5.**

> What's the teacher doing right now?

> She's/He's talking to …

LANGUAGE & BEYOND

PLEASE KEEP OFF THE GRASS

PLEASE NO PETS

Thank you for recycling

PLEASE USE SIDE ENTRANCE

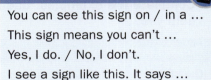

Sorry WE'RE CLOSED

>>> Be polite

SPEAK AND READ

1 🔊 **Work in pairs. Ask and answer the questions.**

1 Where can you see the signs in the pictures?
2 What do they mean?
3 Do you see any signs like these on your way to school? Which ones?

2 Write the polite words from the signs.

please, ...

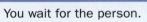

> **PHRASE BYTES**
>
> You can see this sign on / in a ...
>
> This sign means you can't ...
>
> Yes, I do. / No, I don't.
>
> I see a sign like this. It says ...

DO

3 Complete the sentences with the polite phrases.

> please   I'm sorry   thank you   excuse me

1 _____ I'm late.
2 _____ . Can I ask a question?
3 _____ for your help.
4 Can I borrow your pen, _____ ?

4 🔊 **Work in groups. Read the situations. What do you do to be polite?**

1 You're opening a door. Someone's walking behind you.
2 You're sitting on the bus to school. An older person's getting on the bus.
3 You're reading in the school library. Your phone starts ringing.
4 You're walking home. A blind person is standing at the corner.

> **PHRASE BYTES**
>
> You wait for the person.
>
> You ask if the person wants to ...
>
> You ask if the person needs ...
>
> You go / don't talk ...
>
> You help the person to ...

REFLECT

5 Talk about the questions. Then read the REFLECTION POINT .

1 Which of the things in Exercise 4 do you usually do?
2 When is it important to use polite words and phrases?
3 Why do you need to look around you on a bus or train?

> **REFLECTION POINT** «
>
> It's important to be polite when you speak and ask for things. Always think of other people and help them.

EXTEND

6 Work in groups. Complete the tasks.

- Choose a place: a movie theater, a bus, or a park.
- Think of a situation: Someone needs help. Some people are polite. Others aren't polite.
- Mime the scene for the other students. Can they describe what's happening?

SCHOOL SKILLS

>>>> Workbook, page 89

SPEAKING I love acting

SPEAK

1 Work in pairs. Describe the pictures.

PHRASE BYTES

Kelly's carrying …

Frank's listening …

Amy's wearing …

Kelly

LISTEN

2 ▶2.57 Listen to the conversations. Who loves acting?

> 1 **Sara:** Hi, Kelly. Where are you, Ana, and Mary going?
> **Kelly:** We're going to soccer practice. Do you want to come?
> **Sara:** No, thanks. I (1) _____ .
> **Kelly:** Really? I (2) _____ .
>
> 2 **Gina:** Well? Do you like it? I (3) _____ .
> **Frank:** I'm sorry, Gina, but it's hip-hop. I (4) _____ .
> **Gina:** Do you like listening to other kinds of music?
> **Frank:** I (5) _____ . Do you have any salsa?
>
> 3 **Donna:** Hey, Amy. What are you wearing?
> **Amy:** It's a dress for the play. Do you like it?
> **Donna:** I (6) _____ .
> **Amy:** I (7) _____ . You can wear all these amazing clothes.
> **Donna:** I know. Excuse me. I'm late for my class.

Frank

3 a Circle the correct option.

> 1 Sara *likes* / *doesn't like* soccer.
> 2 Kelly *loves* / *hates* soccer.
> 3 Frank *likes* / *doesn't like* the music.
> 4 Frank *loves* / *hates* hip-hop.
> 5 Frank *likes* / *doesn't like* listening to salsa.
> 6 Donna really *likes* / *doesn't like* the colors.

b ▶2.58 Listen and check your answers to Exercise 3a. Then listen and repeat.

Amy

4 ▶2.57 Complete the conversations in Exercise 2. Use your answers to Exercises 2 and 3a to help you. Listen again to check your answers.

5 a Add two things to the list. Then answer for you.

Do you like …		You	Partner
	dancing?		
	classical music?		
	acting?		
	soccer?		

✓✓ I love it.
✓ I like it.
✗ I don't like it.
✗✗ I hate it.

b Work in pairs. Ask and answer the questions in Exercise 5a. Complete the table with your partner's answers.

Do you like … ? *Yes, I do. I love it.* *No, I don't.*

ACT

6 Work in pairs. Complete the tasks.

- You meet a friend after school.
- Write a short conversation. Start with the question: *Hi. Where are you going?*
- Use the conversations in Exercise 2 to help you.
- Present your scene to other students in the class.

PHRASEBOOK ▶2.59

Say you like something

I like music.

I like listening to music.

I love acting / dancing.

I really like …

Say you don't like something

I don't like dancing.

I hate hip-hop.

Questions

Do you like it?

Do you like listening to other kinds of music?

WRITING A day in the city

>>> Write a short message

READ

1 Look at the picture. What's Jen doing?

2 Read the short messages. Where's Jen in each message?

> I'm sitting on the train with Lena. We're going to Manhattan. I love the city. I like walking in the park. I also love watching people.
>
> 55 minutes
>
> ────────────
>
> Lena's shopping. She has a new dress. She also has some new shoes. I'm waiting for her in a café. I'm also waiting for my soda!
>
> 2 minutes

3 Read the tips in the **HOW TO** box. Then underline three sentences with *also* in Jen's message. Circle the similar idea in the sentence before.

HOW TO ❓

use *also*

- Use *also* to add another similar idea.
- Use *also* after *be*.
  I'm also waiting for my soda!
- Use *also* before other verbs.
  I also love watching people.

PRACTICE

4 Rewrite the second sentence using *also*.

1 I like salsa music. (I like classical music.)
  I also like classical music.

2 I have a blue jacket. (I have a blue shirt.)

3 My dad's an actor. (He's a teacher.)

4 I go to dance classes. (I'm studying the violin.)

5 There are two theaters in my city. (There are two movie theaters.)

6 We speak Spanish. (We speak some French.)

DISCUSS

5 Talk about where you like going with a friend. How do you get there? What do you like doing there?

WRITE

6 Write two short text messages during a trip with a friend.

1 Say where you are. What are you doing? Who are you with? What do you love, like, or hate doing in this place?
2 Use present progressive verbs to talk about what you are doing right now when you are texting.
3 Use *also* to add more ideas. See the **HOW TO** box.

SHARE

7 Exchange your text messages with a classmate. Write replies.

>>>> Workbook, pages 88–89

VOCABULARY Clothes

> What can I wear tonight?
>
> 2 minutes ago

1 Write the names of the clothes.

1 ....
2 ....
3 ....
4 ....
5 ....
6 ....
7 ....
8 ....
9 ....
10 ....

___ /10

Action verbs

2 Complete the sentences with the verbs in the box.

carry	dance	drive	fly	point	run
shop	sit	stand	swim	talk	wait

1 .... for the waiter to come.
2 .... at things I want to eat on the menu.
3 .... to Mom on the phone.
4 .... around the yard for exercise.
5 .... my new car.
6 .... for new clothes.
7 .... my shopping bags home.
8 .... to New York in my private plane.
9 .... in a movie theater to watch my new movie.
10 .... in the street for pictures.
11 .... to salsa music.
12 .... in my amazing pool.

___ /12

GRAMMAR Present progressive

3 Write the verbs in the present progressive.

1 I _____ (drive) to the movies.

2 A lot of people _____ (stand) in the street.

3 They _____ (wait) to see me.

4 Now I _____ (talk) to Ronnie Dipp, the famous actor.

5 He _____ (make) a new movie right now.

6 We _____ (sit) in the movie theater.

7 We _____ (have) a fantastic time.

___ /14

Present progressive

4 Complete the questions and short answers with the present progressive.

What (1) _____ now? (you / do)

I'm flying a plane.

Where (2) _____ ? (you / go)

I'm going to London.

(3) _____ alone? (you / fly)

(4) No, I _____ . I'm flying with Ronnie.

(5) _____ with you now? (he / sit)

(6) Yes, he _____ .

Are you having lunch?

(7) No, we _____ .

___ /14

Your score: ___ /50

SKILLS CHECK

✓✓✓	Yes, I can. No problem!
✓✓	Yes, I can. But I need a little help.
✓	Yes, I can. But I need a lot of help.

I can read part of a play. ....
I can listen to descriptions. ....
I can be polite. ....
I can talk about things I like. ....
I can write a short message. ....

WEATHER REPORT

Washington, DC, the USA

IN THE PICTURE World weather

>>> **Talk about the weather**

WORK WITH WORDS Countries, the weather

1 **RECALL** Work in pairs. Write the countries next to the correct continent. Use the map to help you. You have two minutes. (NOTE: Two countries are in two continents.)

| Australia | Brazil | Chile | Germany | Italy | Japan |
| Mexico | Russia | South Africa | the USA | Turkey | |

AFRICA	
ASIA	
AUSTRALIA	*Australia*
EUROPE	
NORTH AMERICA	
SOUTH AMERICA	

Buenos Aires, Argentina

2 a ▶3.01 **Match the words to the weather icons. Then listen and check.**

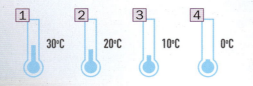

| cloudy _____ | foggy _____ | raining _____ |
| snowing _____ | sunny _____ | windy _____ |

b ▶3.02 **Match the temperatures to the adjectives. Then listen and check.**

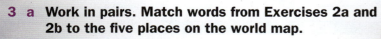

| 1 | 2 | 3 | 4 |
| 30°C | 20°C | 10°C | 0°C |

cold _____
cool _____
hot _____
warm _____

3 a Work in pairs. Match words from Exercises 2a and 2b to the five places on the world map.

b ▶3.03 Listen and check or complete your answers. Then listen and repeat the weather words.

c Choose the correct options to complete the sentences.
1 When it's hot and sunny, it's usually a *wet* / *dry* day.
2 When it's raining or snowing, it's a *wet* / *dry* day.

Moscow, Russia

Tokyo, Japan

Cape Town, South Africa

4 a ▶3.04 **PRONOUNCE** Listen and repeat the /ð/ in _wea**th**er_.

b ▶3.05 Listen and repeat these words.

bro**th**er   fa**th**er   mo**th**er   **th**at   **th**ese   **th**ey   **th**is   **th**ose

5 THE MOVING PICTURE ▶ **Watch the video. What's the weather like in each clip?**

SPEAK

6 a 💭 **Think about your answers to these questions.**

1 What's the weather like today? Is it normal for this time of the year?
2 What's your favorite weather? What weather don't you like?
3 Look at the seasons in the box. Which do you have where you live? What months are they?

autumn   dry season   rainy season
spring   summer   winter

b Work in pairs. Compare your answers to Exercise 6a.

PHRASE BYTES

Today it's …

That's normal for this month / season.

It's usually … at this time of the year.

I like / love … weather.

I don't like / hate it when it's …

MOVE BEYOND

Do the Words & Beyond exercise on page 113.

Workbook, page 92

>>> **Read and take a test**

SPEAK AND READ

1 Work in pairs. Can you remember the things in the box?

> my first teacher   my homework   my last vacation
> new English words   people's birthdays   phone numbers

PHRASE BYTES

I can usually / never remember …

I sometimes forget …

I can't remember …

2 ▶3.06 Take the MEMORY TEST.

3 Now read the explanation for your answers.

MEMORY TEST

HOW GOOD IS YOUR MEMORY? TAKE THIS TEST!

1 Look at this number for five seconds. Close your book. Write it.
5 3 9 1 6 2 4

2 Look at these letters for five seconds. Close your book. Write them.
G K L O F X R

3 Where were you at 6 p.m. yesterday?
4 Who was <u>not</u> in your last class?
5 What was the weather like on Saturday morning?
6 What color was your first backpack?
7 What were the answers to questions 1 and 2? (Don't look!)

EXPLANATION

We have _two_ kinds of memory.
One kind is just for now. It's our "working memory." It can remember about seven things for about 15 seconds. You use it when you add a number to your phone or do a math problem. Questions 1 and 2 test this kind of memory. Count your correct answers.

2 correct = good	0 correct = not so good
1 correct = OK	

Our other memory can remember things for a long time. It's our "long-term memory." You use it when you remember words in English or talk to your friends about last weekend. Questions 3–7 test this kind of memory. Count your correct answers.

5 correct = wow!	2 correct = OK
3–4 correct = good	0–1 correct = not so good

4 **Can you remember? Answer the questions.**

1 How many kinds of memory do we have?
2 How many things can our "working memory" remember? For how long?

PHRASE BYTES

My working memory is / isn't …

I can usually remember … because …

I can't remember … because …

REACT

5 Work in pairs. Do you think you have a good working memory or a good long-term memory? What things are easy for you to remember? Tell your partner.

MOVE BEYOND

Write two more questions for the test – one for "working memory," the other for "long-term memory." Give them to another student to answer.

>>> Describe things in the past

READ AND LISTEN >>> Grammar in context

1 **▶3.07** **Read and listen to the conversation. Ian and Ana were at the same place on Sunday. Where?**

Ian:	Guess where I was this weekend.
Ana:	I don't know. It was a hot day. Were you at the pool?
Ian:	Yes, I was – on Saturday. But I wasn't there yesterday. I was at school.
Ana:	Really? I was there too. I was in a play.
Ian:	I know. I was in the audience. Was it your first play?
Ana:	No, it wasn't.
Ian:	Well, you were really good.
Ana:	Thanks! Were Jack and Paul there?
Ian:	No, they weren't. They were at the pool both days.

STUDY

2 **Complete the examples. Use Exercise 1 to help you.**

Was/were	
Use *was/were* to talk about the past.	
Affirmative	**Negative**
I/he/she/it was	I/he/she/it wasn't
you/we/they were	you/we/they weren't
It _____ a hot day.	But I _____ there yesterday.
They _____ at the pool.	
Questions	**Short answers**
Were **you** at the pool?	Yes, I was.
Jack and Paul _____ there?	No, they _____ .
_____ **it** your first play?	No, it _____ .
Time expressions	
yesterday, on the weekend, on Saturday, last Sunday/weekend/week	

See GRAMMAR DATABASE, page 105.

PRACTICE

3 **a** **Complete the sentences. Use *was* or *were*.**

1	The weather ___was___ good.	True False
2	I _____ at home.	True False
3	My best friends _____ on the internet.	True False
4	I _____ happy.	True False
5	My family and I _____ at the movies.	True False
6	Our English teacher _____ at school.	True False

b **Are the sentences true for you last Saturday afternoon? Circle *True* or *False*.**

c **Correct the false sentences. Use *wasn't* or *weren't*.**

Last Saturday afternoon ...

4 **Answer the questions about your first school. Use short answers.**

1 Was it near your house?
  Yes, it was. / No, it wasn't.
2 Were your best friends in your class?
3 Was it a big school?
4 Were all your teachers women?
5 Was the school cold in the winter?
6 Were you a good student?

5 **Write questions about when you were six years old. Use *was* or *were*.**

1 What / your teacher's name?
  What was your teacher's name?
2 Who / your best friends?
3 your hair / long or short?
4 How old / your parents?
5 you / an only child?
6 What / your favorite food?

SPEAK

6 **Work in pairs. Ask and answer the questions in Exercise 5.**

>>> Listen to a description of a day

WORK WITH WORDS The country

1 a Work in pairs. Match the words in the box to the things in the pictures.

beach _____	forest _____	island _____
mountain _____	ocean _____	river _____
sky _____	town _____	tree _____ village _____

b ▶3.08 Listen and check or complete your answers.

2 ▶3.09 Listen and repeat the country words.

3 Work in pairs. Student A: choose a word from Exercise 1a and say two words or names to describe it. Student B: say the word from Exercise 1a. Then change roles.

Blue, cloudy. *Is it the sky?* *Yes.* *No. Try again.*

LISTEN

4 ▶3.10 Lizzie is describing her weekend. Read the **LISTENING TIP**. Then listen. Which two pictures above are from her weekend?

5 ▶3.10 Listen again. Complete Lizzie's message to another friend, Xenia. Write one, two, or three words in the blanks.

Hi Xenia! I'm back home again after camping in the (1) _____ . (I prefer the (2) _____ , but Mom doesn't like it.) We arrived on (3) _____ evening. The weather was (4) _____ on Saturday morning, but terrible in the afternoon. We went to a town. It was great – dinner in a (5) _____ and a movie. I bought a new (6) _____ !
See you at school, Lizzie

REACT

6 🔄 Work in pairs. Do you prefer the beach or the mountains? Why?

LISTENING TIP ✓
Listen first for the general idea. Don't try to understand everything.

PHRASE BYTES 📖
I prefer ... because you can ...
Really? I don't like ... because ...

MOVE BEYOND »»
Do the Words & Beyond exercise on page 113.

»»» Workbook, pages 96–97

>>> Talk about events in the past

READ AND LISTEN >>> Grammar in context

1 ▶3.11 **Read and listen to the conversation. What can you see in the picture? Who isn't very happy?**

Ben: How was your day off from school?
Tony: I **had** a great time. We **went** to Sky Park.
Ben: But it **rained** all day.
Tony: It **stopped** in the afternoon. There weren't many people, so we **tried** everything. We **went** on the big roller coaster too. And guess what? We **saw** Harry there. He **came** on the roller coaster with us. Look, they **took** this picture. It's so good I **bought** one for me and one for Harry.
Ben: He isn't very happy!
Tony: No. He **hated** it!

STUDY

2 **Complete the examples. Use Exercise 1 to help you.**

Simple past
Affirmative regular verbs
rain > It _rained_ all day.
hate > He _____ it!
Spelling
stop > It _____ in the afternoon.
try > We _____ everything.

See GRAMMAR DATABASE, page 105.

3 **Find the simple past of the irregular verbs in Exercise 1.**

1 buy _bought_   4 have _____
2 come _____   5 see _____
3 go _____   6 take _____

4 ▶3.12 PRONOUNCE **Listen and repeat the simple past verbs in Exercises 2 and 3.**

>>> Workbook, page 98

PRACTICE

5 ▶3.13 **Complete the conversation with the simple past form of the regular verbs. Then listen and check your answers.**

Tony: How was *your* day off from school?
Ben: Not good.
Tony: Why?
Ben: Well, I had some exams this week, so I (1) _stayed_ (stay) home in the morning and I (2) _____ (study). I (3) _____ (chat) with Will on the internet, but only because I (4) _____ (need) some help. In the afternoon Lewis and I (5) _____ (play) a game online. I (6) _____ (like) that. But then we (7) _____ (visit) my cousins. They're really young, and it was boring. When we (8) _____ (arrive) home, it was time for bed!

6 **Write the simple past of the regular and irregular verbs. Then complete the rest of the information about your great day out.**

MY GREAT DAY OUT

1 I _went_ (go) to _the beach_ (place).
2 I _____ (get) there by _____ (transportation).
3 _____ (people) _____ (come) with me.
4 The weather _____ (be) _____ (adjective).
5 We _____ (have) _____ (food) for lunch and _____ (food) for dinner.
6 I _____ (take) pictures of _____ (person/thing/place).
7 I _____ (see) _____ (person/thing/place).
8 I _____ (buy) _____ (souvenir/postcard/snack).

SPEAK

7 a **Prepare to talk about your great day out. Practice your sentences from Exercise 6.**

b **Work in pairs. Tell your partner about your great day out. Try not to look at your sentences.**

LANGUAGE & BEYOND

I want some watermelon and some water. I have $1.

I want some pasta salad and a banana. I have $2.50.

I want a cheese sandwich, an apple, and some juice. I have $2.

bananas	25¢	pasta salad	$1.90	
apples	20¢	water	60¢	
watermelon	20¢	juice	95¢	
sandwiches	$1.75			
(chicken, cheese, or egg)				

Lucy   Maria   Jake

>>> Be careful with money

SPEAK AND READ

1 It's the morning recess at school. Lucy, Maria, and Jake want to buy some food. Work in pairs and answer the questions.

(Note: 1 dollar [$] = 100 cents [¢])
1 How much is their food?
2 Can they buy it with their money?
3 How much is the change (= money back)?

DO

2 Work in pairs. You go to a store. Put the money tips in the best order, from 1 to 5. Compare your answers.

.... Check your change.
.... Not enough money? Choose again.
.... Do the math. How much do you need?

.... Look at how much money you have.
.... Decide what you want.

3 a 📖 You're at Lucy, Maria, and Jake's school. You have $1.50 for a morning snack and $3.50 for lunch. Answer the questions.

1 What do you want for your snack and for lunch?
2 How much money do you need?
3 How much change do you get?

b 📖 Work in pairs. Tell your partner your decisions. Check your partner's math.

PHRASE BYTES 📱

Sandwiches are one dollar and seventy-five cents, and water is …

One dollar and seventy-five cents plus (+) sixty cents is …

Three dollars and fifty cents minus (−) … is …

That's right / wrong.

REFLECT

4 Talk about the questions. Then read the **REFLECTION POINT**.

1 When do you need to buy things?
2 Do you always follow the tips in Exercise 2? Why or why not?
3 Why is it important to follow these tips?

REFLECTION POINT

It's important to be careful with money. Know how much you have and how much you need. Always check your change.

EXTEND

5 Work in pairs. You have $10 each and want to buy a birthday present for a friend.

- Do you want to buy two smaller presents or one big one with $20?
- Think of some presents. How much do they cost? Choose what to buy.

SCHOOL SKILLS

>>>> Workbook, page 101

>>> **Ask how people are**

SPEAK

1 Work in pairs. Look at the pictures. How do you think the people feel – good or bad?

LISTEN

2 ▶3.14 Listen to the conversations. Check your answers to Exercise 1.

1
Holly: Hi, Dean.
Dean: Hi, Holly. (1) _____
Holly: OK. How are you?
Dean: Not too bad.

2
Mr. Sims: Hello, Jay. (2) _____
Jay: I'm fine, thanks. And you?
Mr. Sims: I'm very well, thank you.

3 ▶3.14 Complete the conversations with the questions in the box. Then listen again and check your answers.

And you?	How's it going?
How are things?	How are you?

4 Read the explanation. Then look at the conversations in Exercise 2 and answer the questions.

> **BE POLITE**
> **Use polite language when:**
> you don't know somebody well.
> it's a formal situation.

3
Dana: Hi, Cindy.
Cindy: Hello, Dana. (3) _____
Dana: Good. (4) _____
Cindy: Not too good.
Dana: Really? Why's that?
Cindy: I don't feel very well.
Dana: Why don't you go home?
Cindy: Yeah, good idea.

1 In which conversation do the people use polite language? How do you know?
2 What polite questions do they use? Can you use these questions with everybody?
3 Which questions can you only use with friends?

5 ▶3.15 Listen and repeat the questions and answers.

ACT

6 📖 Work in pairs. Complete the tasks.
- Prepare two scenes at school: one scene with two friends, the other with a student and a teacher.
- In the scenes the people say "hello" and ask how the other person is.
- Practice your scenes. Then present them to other students.

PHRASEBOOK ▶3.16

Ask how people are

How are you?

How are things?

How's it going?

And you?

Say how you are

Good.

Not too bad.

I'm fine (thanks).

I'm very well (thank you).

Not too good.

WRITING Send me a postcard

>>> Write a postcard

SPEAK AND READ

1 Work in pairs. How often do you send postcards? How often do you get them? When was the last time?

2 Read the postcard. (Don't worry about the mistakes!) Why wasn't yesterday a perfect day?

Hi from Long Beach!

We **arriveed** here on Friday night. The **vilage** is really nice, and **theirs** a great beach, of course! The weather's hot and **suny**, but the ocean is really cold. Yesterday we went to a little island **four** a picnic, but Dad took the wrong bag, so we only **staied** until lunchtime.

See you next week.

Sonia

3 Read the tips in the **HOW TO** box. Then correct the spelling of the words in bold in the postcard.

> **HOW TO** ?
>
> check your spelling
>
> - Check for double letters: *arrive* (NOT ~~arive~~), *summer* (NOT ~~sumer~~).
> - Check verbs: *tried* (NOT ~~tryed~~), *enjoyed* (NOT ~~enjoied~~).
> - Check words with the same pronunciation: *there/their*, *it's/its*.

PRACTICE

4 **Choose the correct spelling of each word.**
 1 Yesterday we *visited / visitted* a town in the mountains.
 2 We *stoped / stopped* for lunch on the way.
 3 It was a *fogy / foggy* day.
 4 It was very cold *too / two* .
 5 I hope you're *having / haveing* better weather.
 6 *Write / Right* soon!

DISCUSS

5 Talk about a visit to a city in a different country or in your country. Describe the place and the weather. What did you do there?

WRITE

6 **Write a postcard from another place.**

> 1 Write where you are. When did you arrive? What interesting things are in this place? Write about an interesting thing you did yesterday.
> 2 Use past tense verbs when you talk about yesterday. Start your postcard with a greeting from the place and finish with a closing sentence and your name.
> 3 Check your spelling. See the **HOW TO** box.

SHARE

7 Read your postcard to other students. Vote on who had the most fun trip.

VOCABULARY The weather

1 Complete the weather words.

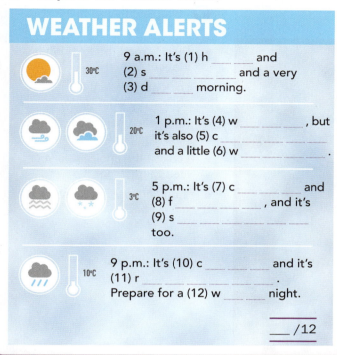

WEATHER ALERTS

9 a.m.: It's (1) h_____ and
(2) s_____ and a very
(3) d_____ morning.

1 p.m.: It's (4) w_____, but
it's also (5) c_____
and a little (6) w_____.

5 p.m.: It's (7) c_____ and
(8) f_____, and it's
(9) s_____
too.

9 p.m.: It's (10) c_____ and it's
(11) r_____.
Prepare for a (12) w_____ night.

___ /12

The country

2 Match the words in the box to the things in the picture.

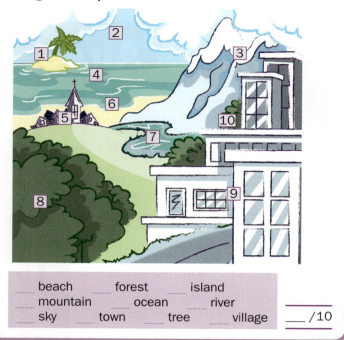

beach	forest	island
mountain	ocean	river
sky	town	tree	village

___ /10

GRAMMAR Was/were

3 Complete the TV interview with *was/wasn't* and *were/weren't*.

Presenter: I'm talking to Judy Murray about the bad weather yesterday. Judy, (1) _____ it bad when you started walking?

Judy: No, it (2) _____ .

Presenter: (3) _____ you prepared for bad weather?

Judy: No, we (4) _____ . And it changed very fast.

Presenter: What (5) _____ the weather like?

Judy: Terrible. We (6) _____ really nervous.

Presenter: Judy, thanks for talking to us.

___ /12

Simple past

4 Complete the news story with the simple past form of the verbs.

Judy Murray and her family (1) _____ (**start**) walking at 10 a.m. in good weather. They (2) _____ (**buy**) sandwiches in a local store, and at 1 p.m. they (3) _____ (**stop**) walking and they (4) _____ (**have**) lunch high up in the mountains. That's when the snow (5) _____ (**come**). At 5 p.m. Judy (6) _____ (**call**) the police for help. Two teams of police officers (7) _____ (**go**) to find them. It was 9 p.m. when they finally (8) _____ (**take**) the family back home.

___ /16

Your score: ___ /50

SKILLS CHECK

✓✓✓	Yes, I can. No problem!
✓✓	Yes, I can. But I need a little help.
✓	Yes, I can. But I need a lot of help.

I can read and take a test. _____
I can listen to a description of a day out. _____
I can be careful with money. _____
I can ask how people are. _____
I can write a postcard. _____

READ

1 Read the blog post about Buenos Aires. Choose the best word (A, B, or C) for each blank.

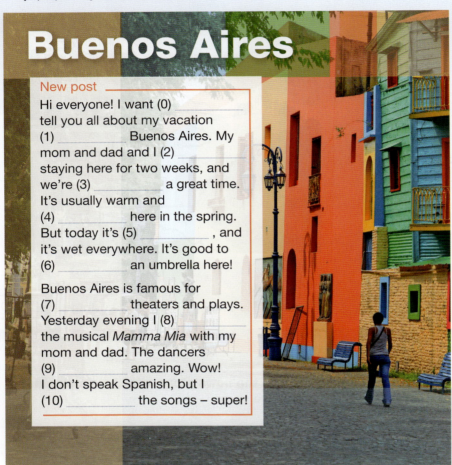

Buenos Aires

New post

Hi everyone! I want (0) .... tell you all about my vacation (1) .... Buenos Aires. My mom and dad and I (2) .... staying here for two weeks, and we're (3) .... a great time. It's usually warm and (4) .... here in the spring. But today it's (5) .... , and it's wet everywhere. It's good to (6) .... an umbrella here!

Buenos Aires is famous for (7) .... theaters and plays. Yesterday evening I (8) .... the musical *Mamma Mia* with my mom and dad. The dancers (9) .... amazing. Wow! I don't speak Spanish, but I (10) .... the songs – super!

TEST-TAKING TIPS

? complete blanks in a text with multiple-choice answers

■ Quickly read the text. What's it about?

■ Look at the example. It shows you what to do.

■ Read each sentence. Do you have an idea for the blank?

■ Look at the choices. Is your idea there?

■ If not, choose the best word.

Example:

0	**A** not	**B** for	**C** to
1	**A** at	**B** in	**C** on
2	**A** am	**B** is	**C** are
3	**A** have	**B** having	**C** had
4	**A** sunny	**B** foggy	**C** windy
5	**A** hot	**B** raining	**C** dry
6	**A** point	**B** shop	**C** carry
7	**A** their	**B** his	**C** its
8	**A** saw	**B** went	**C** had
9	**A** was	**B** were	**C** weren't
10	**A** hated	**B** listened	**C** loved

Reading: _____ /10

LISTEN

2 ▶ 3.17 **Listen to five conversations. You will hear each conversation twice. Choose the correct answer for each question (A, B, or C). Then listen again.**

Example:

0 Where was Peter yesterday?

A B C

1 What's Bella's favorite music?

A B C

2 What's Jacob doing?

A B C

3 How old is Kira's sister?

A B C

4 What's on the floor?

A B C

5 How much is Lucy's lunch?

A $2.00 — Thank you for shopping with us!
B $2.95 — Thank you for shopping with us!
C $2.05 — Thank you for shopping with us!

Listening: _____ / 10

WRITE

3 **Read the descriptions and complete the country words.**

Example:

0 This long area of water goes to the ocean. r i v e r

1 It's a very small town in the country. v _____

2 It's very high, and it often has snow on it. m _____

3 It's near the ocean, and people often lie on it in the sun. b _____

4 It's an area of land with water all around it. i _____

5 There are lots of trees in it. f _____

_____ /5

4 **Read the message from your friend Aiden. Write a reply. Tell him what you're doing (25–35 words).**

> Hi, I'm bored! Are you at home? What are you doing now? Do you want to come over to my house and play computer games?

_____ /5

Writing: _____ / 10

Progress check score _____ /30

Pronouns

Personal pronouns and possessive adjectives

		Personal pronouns	Possessive adjectives
Singular	I	my
	you	your
	he	his
	she	her
	it	its
Plural	we	our
	you	your
	they	their

Be

- Notice how we use the verb *be*:
  Hi, I'm Sarah.
  He isn't in our class.
  Where are your parents from?

Affirmative

I'm
You're
He's/She's/It's
We're/They're

Negative

I'm not
You aren't
He/She/It isn't
We/They aren't

Questions and short answers

Am I … ?	Yes, you are. / No, you're not.
Are you … ?	Yes, I am. / No, I'm not.
Is he … ?	Yes, he is. / No, he isn't.
Is she … ?	Yes, she is. / No, she isn't.
Is it … ?	Yes, it is. / No, it isn't.
Are we … ?	Yes, you are. / No, you're not.
Are they … ?	Yes, they are. /No, they aren't.

Plural nouns

- Add -s to most nouns in the plural:
  games, movies, hotels
- Add -es to nouns ending in -ch, -sh, -s, -ss, or -x:
  buses, classes, lunches, boxes
- For nouns ending in a consonant and *y*, change *y* to *i* and add -es: *city – cities*
- For nouns ending in a vowel and *y*, add -s:
  key – keys
- The following nouns are always plural:
  jeans, sunglasses, scissors
- The following nouns have irregular plural forms:
  man – **men**   person – **people**
  woman – **women**   child – **children**
  foot – **feet**   mouse – **mice**
  fish – **fish**

a/an, the

USE

- Use *a/an* when you mention a noun for the first time:
  *I like **an** ice-cream cone on a hot day.*
- Use *a/an* with nouns for jobs and occupations:
  *We have **a** great math teacher.*
- Use *the* before a specific thing:
  ***The** school bus is late.*
- Use *the* before something there is only one of:
  *I love **the** internet.*
- Use no article when talking about things in general:
  I don't like video games.

FORM

- Use *a* before nouns beginning with consonant sounds: *a bus*
- Use *an* before nouns beginning with vowel sounds: *an ice-cream cone*

This/that, these/those

	Here	There
Singular	this	that
Plural	these	those

- Use *this* to talk about one thing here:
  What's this?
- Use *these* to talk about more than one thing here: *These bananas are yellow.*
- Use *that* to talk about one thing there:
  That apple is red.
- Use *those* to talk about more than one thing there: *I like those T-shirts.*

Have

USE

- Use *have* to talk about possession:
  I **have** one brother.
  I **don't have** a tablet.
  Sam **has** a computer.
  Do you **have** a favorite TV show?

FORM

Affirmative

I **have**	
You **have**	
He/She/It **has**	a big family.
We **have**	
They **have**	

Negative

I **don't have**	
You **don't have**	
He/She/It **doesn't have**	a cell phone.
We **don't have**	
They **don't have**	

- You often use *any* with the negative forms of *have* and plural nouns:
  I don't have **any apples**.

Questions and short answers

Do	I/you/we/they	**have** a tablet?
Does	he/she/it	**have** a cell phone?

Yes,	you/I/we/they	**do.**
	he/she/it	**does.**
No,	you/I/we/they	**don't.**
	he/she/it	**doesn't.**

- You often use *any* before plural nouns with the question forms of *have*:
  Do you have **any** brothers or sisters?

Whose?; possessive 's/s' and possessive pronouns

Whose? and possessive 's/s'

USE

- Use possessive 's and *whose* to talk about possessions or relationships:
  Whose phone is this?
  It's my sister's. (The phone belongs to my sister.)
  Whose keys are these?
  They're my dad's.

FORM

- Use singular noun + 's:
  It's my sister's phone. (sister + 's + phone)
- Use regular plural noun + s':
  That's my grandparents' house over there. (grandparent + s' + house)
- Use 's for irregular plural nouns such as *children, people, women, men*:
  The children's books were on the floor.

WATCH OUT! Notice the difference between possessive 's and the contraction of *is* – 's:
Is that Jacob's bag?
Jacob's 14 years old.

Possessive pronouns

USE

- Use a possessive pronoun in place of a possessive adjective (*my, your*) + noun:
  It's her book. It's **hers**.
  That's my phone. It's **mine**.

FORM

Possessive adjectives	Possessive pronouns
my	mine
your	yours
his/her	his/hers
our	ours
their	theirs

Imperatives and object pronouns

Imperatives

USE

- Use imperatives to give instructions and commands:
  Give them food and water every day.
  Come into the classroom and **sit** down.

FORM

- Form the imperative with the base form of the verb:
  Open the window.
  Close the door.
- Use *don't* before the verb to tell someone not to do something:
  Shhhh! **Don't talk.**
  Don't forget to give them food and water.

Object pronouns

USE

- Use object pronouns after verbs:
  Listen to **me.**
  Give **them** food and water every day.
  Don't put **her** in your room.

FORM

Subject pronouns	Object pronouns
I	me
you	you
he	him
she	her
it	it
we	us
you	you
they	them

There is / there are

USE

- Use *there is / there are* to describe what's in a place:
  There's a big clock in my classroom.
  There isn't a computer.
  There are some pictures on the wall.
  Is there a table?

FORM

Affirmative

There's a desk.
There are some chairs.

- *There's* is the contraction of *there is.* You usually use the contraction in informal English.
- You often use *some* with *there are* before plural nouns.

Negative

There isn't a computer.
There aren't any windows.

- You often use *any* with *there aren't* before plural nouns.
- *There isn't* and *there aren't* are the short forms of *there is not* and *there are not.* You usually use the short forms in informal English.

Questions and short answers

Is there a clock?	Yes, **there is.** / No, **there isn't.**
Are there any pictures?	Yes, **there is.** / No, **there aren't.**

Can/can't

USE

- Use *can/can't* to talk about the things we have the ability or time to do:
  *I **can** play tennis.*
  *I **can't** hear very well.*

FORM

- The form stays the same. *Can and can't* are the same for *I, you, he/she/it, we,* and *they.*

I		
You		
He/She/It	can/can't	see you.
We		
They		

Questions and short answers

- Form questions by changing the word order:
  ***Can you** play the guitar?*

Can	I/you/we/they	swim?	Yes, I/you/we/they **can**.
			No, I/you/we/they **can't**.
	he/she/it		Yes, he/she/it **can**.
			No, he/she/it **can't**.

Simple present

USE

Use the simple present to talk about
- things that are generally true:
  *My sister **plays** the violin.*
  *Max **writes** the songs for our group.*
- habits and routines:
  *I **practice** the piano every day.*
  *We **watch** television at night.*

FORM

Affirmative

- The simple present for *I, you, we,* and *they* is the same. For the *he/she/it* forms, add *-s, -es,* or *-ies* to the verb.

I/You/We/They	read	a lot of books.
He/She/It	plays	soccer every weekend.

Spelling: *he/she/it* forms

- If a verb ends in *-ch, -s, -sh, -x,* or *-o,* add *-es:*
  *My aunt **teaches** English at a school.*
  *Ingrid **goes** to a music club after school.*
- If a verb ends in a consonant and *-y,* change the *-y* to *-i* and add *-es:*
  *My brother **studies** Spanish.*

Simple present

FORM
Negative

- Form the simple present negative with *don't* (*do not*) or *doesn't* (*does not*) + verb.

I/You/We/They	**don't**	watch television	in the morning.
He/She/It	**doesn't**	play soccer	after school.

> **WATCH OUT!** In negative sentences don't add **-s** to the verb after **doesn't**:
> *He doesn't* **speak** *French. (not* ~~He doesn't speaks French.~~*)*

Questions and short answers

- Form questions in the simple present with *do/ does* + subject + verb.

Do	I/you/we/they	**believe** her?
Does	he/she/it	**work** at a school?

Yes,	I/you/we/they	**do.**
	he/she/it	**does.**
No,	I/you/we/they	**don't.**
	he/she/it	**doesn't.**

Question words

- To ask questions in the simple present, use a question word (*where, who, what, when, how, which, why*) + *do/does* + subject + verb:
When do you go to bed?
How do you get to school?

Adverbs of frequency

USE

- Use adverbs of frequency to say how often you do things:
I **usually** *take the bus to school.*
We **sometimes** *watch movies at night.*
My sister **never** *gets up early.*

- The main adverbs of frequency are (in order of frequency):

0%	never
	sometimes
	often
	usually
100%	always

- Adverbs of frequency usually go **before** the main verb:
I **sometimes help** *my dad with the cooking.*
- Adverbs of frequency go **after** am/are/is/can:
Her room **is always** *a mess.*
- Look at where the adverbs go in these questions:
What time do you **usually** *get up?*
How **often** *do you have lunch at school?*

Comparative adjectives

USE

- Use comparative adjectives to compare two things:
*New York is **bigger than** Washington, DC.*
*Washington, DC is **more dangerous than** New York.*

FORM

- To form the comparative of most adjectives, add -er.
- Most longer adjectives (e.g., *expensive*) add *more* before the adjective:
*New York is **more** expensive than Chicago.*
- See the table for other spelling changes.
- Use *than* after the comparative adjective:
*Washington, DC, is smaller **than** New York.*

Word type	Adjective	Comparative adjective
One syllable	clean	clean**er**
One syllable ending in -e	safe	safe**r**
One syllable ending in one vowel + one consonant	big	bi**gger**
Two syllables ending in -y	dirty	dirt**ier**
Two or more syllables	expensive	**more** expensive
Two or more syllables ending in -er, -et, -ow, or -le	quiet	quiet**er**

WATCH OUT! Some comparative adjectives are irregular.

Adjective	Comparative adjective
good	better
bad	worse
far	further/farther

Some and *any*, *much* and *many*

Countable nouns

- are nouns you can count:
fact, vegetable, girl
- use *a/an* or *the* in the singular:
I usually eat an apple every day.
- have a singular and a plural form:
lemon   lemons

Uncountable nouns

- are nouns you can't count:
meat, cheese, pasta
- don't have a plural from:
*I like a lot of **cheese** on my pasta.*
- You can't say *one meat, two meats.*
- Some more common uncountable nouns are *food, salad, bread, spaghetti, soup, milk, juice, fruit, rice.*
- Some nouns can be both countable and uncountable:
How much fruit do you eat?
Papaya is a tropical fruit.

Some

USE

- Use *some* to describe an amount that is not big and not small. You can use *some* with countable and uncountable nouns:
*We have **some bananas**.*
*There's **some juice** in the refrigerator.*
- You can also use *some* when making offers or requests with countable and uncountable nouns:
*Would you like **some fries**?*
*Can I have **some pasta**?*

Any

USE

- Use *any* in negative sentences to talk about zero amounts. You can use *any* with both countable and uncountable nouns:
*There aren't **any vegetables**.*
*We don't have **any bread**.*
- Use *any* with countable and uncountable nouns to ask about quantity:
*Do we have **any milk**?*
*Are there **any eggs** in the refrigerator?*

Much and *many*

USE

- Use *How many* or *How much* to ask about quantity. Use *How many* for countable nouns and *How much* for uncountable nouns:
***How many** minutes do you cook pasta?*
***How much** pasta do Italians eat?*
- Use *not + many* with countable nouns and *not + much* with uncountable nouns to talk about a small amount of something in negative sentences:
*Italians don't eat **much** meat.*
*There aren't **many** eggs in the refrigerator.*

Present progressive

USE

- Use the present progressive to talk about things in progress now or around now:
  *What **are you doing**?*
  *I'm **watching** television.*
  *It's very sunny, so my brother **is wearing** sunglasses.*
- You often use time expressions such as *now, today, at the moment*, and *right now* with the present progressive:
  *I'm **not studying** today. It's a holiday.*

FORM

Affirmative

- Form the present progressive with *be + -ing* form of the verb.

I'm You're He's/She's	wearing	sneakers.
It's	raining.	
We're They're	sleeping.	

- You usually use the short forms of *be* in the present progressive:
  *He's **riding** his bike.*

Spelling

- If a verb ends in *-e*, remove the final *-e* before adding *-ing*:
  take – taking   use – using
- If a verb ends in a vowel (e.g., *i, a, o*) and a consonant (e.g., *m, p, t*), double the consonant before adding *-ing*:
  swim – swimming   shop – shopping
- If a verb ends in *-ie*, change the *-ie* to *-ying*:
  lie – lying

Negative

- Form the present progressive negative with *be + not + -ing* form of the verb.

I'm not You aren't He isn't / She isn't	watching	a video.
It isn't	working.	
We aren't They aren't	meeting	friends.

Questions and short answers

- Form present progressive questions with *be + subject + -ing* form of the verb.

Am	I	listening to music?	Yes, you **are**. / No, you're **not**.
Are	you		Yes, I **am**. / No, I'm **not**.
Is	he/she	making a cake?	Yes, he/she **is**. / No, he/she **isn't**.
Is	it	raining?	Yes, it **is**. / No, it **isn't**.
Are	we/they	having a party?	Yes, we/they **are**. / No, we/they **aren't**.

- You can also use question words (*What, Why, Who, Where, How*) before *be*:
  ***What are you doing** here?*
  ***Why are you wearing** a shirt and jacket?*
  ***Where are you going**?*

> **WATCH OUT!** Never use contractions in affirmative short answers:
> *Yes, **I am**. (not ~~Yes, I'm.~~)*

Was/were

- Use the simple past of *be* to talk about situations in the past:
  *I **was** in a play on Saturday. My parents **were** in the audience.*
  *My sister **wasn't** at school yesterday.*

FORM

Affirmative

- The affirmative form of the simple past of *be* is *was* or *were*.

I/He/She/It	**was**	
You/We/They	**were**	late for school.

Negative

- The negative form of the simple past of *be* is *wasn't* or *weren't*.

I/He/She/It	**wasn't** (was not)	at school
You/We/They	**weren't** (were not)	yesterday.

Questions and short answers

- To form questions, use *was/were* + subject.

Were you		Yes, I **was**. No, I **wasn't**.
Was he/she/it	at the pool yesterday?	Yes, he/she/it **was**. No, he/she/it **wasn't**.
Were we/they		Yes, we/they **were**. No, we/they **weren't**.

- You often use these time expressions with *was/were*:

yesterday, on Saturday, last Sunday/weekend/ week

Simple past

- Use the simple past to talk about completed actions in the past:
  *Yesterday I **went** to the beach and **swam** in the ocean.*
  *In the evening I **ate** dinner and **watched** TV.*

- You often use these time expressions with the simple past:

yesterday	last night/week/month/year	
on Monday	in October	in 2013

FORM

Regular verbs

- Form the simple past of regular verbs with verb + *-ed*. It is the same for all persons.

I/You/He/She/It/We/They	**hated** it.

Spelling

- If a verb ends in *-y*, change the *y* to *i* before adding *-ed*:
  *study – stud**ied***
- But not if there is a vowel before the *-y*:
  *play – play**ed*** (not ~~plaied~~)
- If a verb ends in a vowel (e.g., *o*) and a consonant (e.g., *p, t*), double the consonant:
  *stop – stop**ped***

Irregular verbs

- Many verbs are irregular in the simple past. You have to learn these.
  *buy – **bought**   come – **came**   go – **went***

See page 114 for a list of irregular verbs in the simple past.

WORDS & BEYOND

Page 10 and 11
MY THINGS

backpack	game console	laptop	phone	sunglasses
bike	ice cream	notebook	sandwich	T-shirt
car	jeans	orange	soccer ball	website

WORK WITH WORDS »»

TIP: Make a dictionary. Write new words with the same first letter together.

TASK: Choose a letter and write three words under it. Next to each word, write the word in your language.

CATEGORIES
clothes
food
games
school
technology
transportation

MOVE BEYOND
Make a *likes* ☺ and *dislikes* ☹ list. Add one word from each category to your lists.

Page 14
COUNTRIES AND NATIONALITIES

Brazil	Brazilian
Germany	German
Italy	Italian
Japan	Japanese
South Africa	South African
Turkey	Turkish

MOVE BEYOND
Think of a famous person or place for each country. Write a sentence.
… *is from/in* [country].
… *is* [nationality].
1 _____
2 _____
3 _____
4 _____
5 _____
6 _____

OTHER IMPORTANT WORDS

album	chair	grape	noisy	story
alphabet	city	great	old	the same
apple	classmate	horrible	point	the UK
article	computer	international	postcards	the USA
bad	cool	internet	quiet	thing
basketball	drink	label	Russia	tourist
big	eat	laptop	similar	trash
boring	favorite	mountain bike	small	vacation
box	fruit salad	neighbor	something	visit
card	game	new	stay (in a hotel)	wastebasket
category	glass	nice		

Page 20

RECALL

OPPOSITE ADJECTIVES

bad	new	same
big	nice	small
different	noisy	young
good	old	
horrible	quiet	

WORK WITH WORDS »»

TIP: Learn opposites together.   **TASK:** Find opposites for these words in the unit: *wrong* – ... , *easy* – ... .

Pages 20 and 21

FAMILY

brother
dad
father
grandchild
grandfather
grandma
grandmother
grandpa
mom
mother
only child
sister

MOVE BEYOND
Make a family tree with these family words.

Grandpa   Grandma   Grandfather   Grandmother

Mother   Father

Brother   Sister

Page 24

PARTS OF THE BODY

arm
back
ear
eye
face
foot
hand
head
leg
mouth
nose
teeth

MOVE BEYOND
Touch and say the parts of your body in the list.

OTHER IMPORTANT WORDS

camera	idea	on the right/left	repeat	tablet
contact list	in the middle	pen	smart	text message
easy	internet	picture	smile	time
fantastic	laptop	player	special	today
friendly	like (adv)	present	spell	vacation
hard	morning	problem	street	wrong number
hear				

WORDS &BEYOND

Page 32

RECALL

PARTS OF THE BODY
arm
back
ear
eye
face
head
leg
mouth
nose
teeth

WORK WITH WORDS »»

TIP: Draw pictures to help you remember new words.

TASK: Draw pictures of the parts of the body.

Pages 32 and 33

PET ANIMALS
bird
cat
chicken
dog
fish
hamster
horse
mouse
rabbit
turtle

MOVE BEYOND
Match these adjectives to the pet animals:
big
horrible
nice
noisy
quiet
small
tall

Page 36

THINGS IN YOUR ROOM
Parts of a room
door
floor
wall
window
Furniture
bed
chair
desk
table
Other things
clock
computer
light
picture

MOVE BEYOND
Add one more word to each category. Use a dictionary to help you.

OTHER IMPORTANT WORDS

adopt	egg	neighbor	refrigerator	tall
basketball	fetch	order	Scottish	touch
borrow	grass	popular	shake hands	the United States
box	homework planner	postcard	stay	wait
cartoon	lunch	quickly	survey	
cross (v)	neat			

Page 42

RECALL

FREE-TIME WORDS

bike
book
friends
internet
movies
music
shopping
soccer
television
video games

WORK WITH WORDS ⟫

TIP: Write a translation (= the word in your language) for new words. Note if the translation is the same, similar, or different.

TASK: Write a translation for the RECALL words. Then write *the same*, *similar*, or *different* next to the translations.

Pages 42 and 43

FREE-TIME ACTIVITIES

go on the internet
go shopping
go to the movies
listen to music
meet friends
play soccer
play video games
read a book
ride my bike
watch television

MOVE BEYOND
Choose five activities. Write a sentence to say when you do them.

Page 46

MUSIC

Musical instruments
drums
guitar
keyboard
piano
violin

Types of music
classical
hip-hop
Latin
pop
rock

MOVE BEYOND
Match some of the words to a famous person or group.

OTHER IMPORTANT WORDS

audio book	deaf	hearing aid	make a note of	singer
blind	diary	homework	movie theater	title
board	disability	influence	piece of paper	touch
dance	due	interview	sign language	walk
dark	headings	light (adj)	sing	wheelchair

Page 54

RECALL

PLACES

farm
hospital
hotel
restaurant
school
soccer stadium
soccer team
store
theater

WORK WITH WORDS »»

TIP: Think of places and people you know.

TASK: How many of the places are there in your city? Make a list and write the names of the places. Do you know people who work in any of the places?

Pages 54 and 55

JOBS

actor
cook
doctor
farmer
nurse
receptionist
sales clerk
soccer player
teacher
waiter/waitress

MOVE BEYOND

Choose five jobs. Write one thing that each person needs.

waiter – a menu

Page 58

DAILY ACTIVITIES

do my homework
finish school
get up
go home
go to bed
go to school
have breakfast
have dinner
have lunch
take a shower
watch TV

MOVE BEYOND

Write your daily routine backwards. Start with the last thing you do and end with the first thing. Don't look at the list of words.

I go to bed …

OTHER IMPORTANT WORDS

active	daily routine	mystery	radio show
believe	drive	normal	smile
carefully	ice cream	order (food in a restaurant)	start
count	mostly	questionnaire	website post
create			

Page 64

RECALL

THINGS IN YOUR ROOM

bed
chair
clock
computer
desk
door
floor
light
picture
table
wall
window

WORK WITH WORDS >>>

TIP: Close your eyes and "see" a place in your head. "Say" the words in your head for all the things in English.

TASK: Close your eyes and "see" your room at home. "Say" the words in your head.

Pages 64 and 65

HOMES

apartment	house
balcony	kitchen
bathroom	living room
bedroom	swimming pool
dining room	terrace
hall	yard

MOVE BEYOND
Write two sentences about your favorite room in your home. Say why you like it.

Page 68

FOOD AND DRINK

apple	lemon
banana	meat
bread	milk
cheese	oil
chicken	pasta
coffee	pizza
egg	rice
fish	salad
fruit	sandwich
fruit salad	steak
grapes	tea
ice cream	vegetables
juice	watermelon

MOVE BEYOND
Write a menu with your favorite food and drinks.

OTHER IMPORTANT WORDS

any	dangerous	far	meal	some
boat	dirty	freezer	much	souvenir
cabinet	Europe	How much is it?	the Netherlands	tall
capital (city)	exchange	kilo	outside	tent
clean	expensive	Latin America	refrigerator	view
comfortable	fact	many	safe	yard
course				

Page 76

RECALL

COLORS

black
blue
brown
green
orange
pink
purple
red
white
yellow

CLOTHES AND ACCESSORIES

bag
jeans
sunglasses
T-shirt

WORK WITH WORDS

TIP: Use colors to organize vocabulary. Write nouns in one color, adjectives in another color, verbs in another, and so on.

TASK: Write *Nouns*, *Verbs*, and *Adjectives* at the top of a piece of paper in different colors. Write four words under each title in the same colors.

Pages 76 and 77

CLOTHES

dress
hat
jacket
pants
shirt
shoes
skirt
sneakers
socks
sweatshirt

MOVE BEYOND

What clothes do you have? How many? Make a list and include colors.

I have a / some / a lot of …

Page 80

ACTION VERBS

carry
chat
dance
drive
fly
point
run
shop
sit
stand
swim
talk
wait
wear

MOVE BEYOND

Use the verbs to write six sentences about things you *always*, *often*, *sometimes*, and *never* do.

OTHER IMPORTANT WORDS

accessories	king	polite	scene	stripes
castle	message	prince	sign	wear
go out	mime	queen	soda	Wow!
guard	play (n)			

Page 86

COUNTRIES
Argentina
Australia
Brazil
Chile
Germany
Italy
Japan
Mexico
Russia
South Africa
the USA
Turkey

CONTINENTS
Africa
Asia
Australia
Europe
North America
South America

WORK WITH WORDS

TIP: Make a note of word stress: **_Ger_**many

TASK: Make a note of word stress in the names of other countries. Use your dictionary for help.

Pages 86 and 87

THE WEATHER
cloudy
cold
cool
dry
foggy
hot
raining
snowing
sunny
warm
wet
windy

MOVE BEYOND
Choose six words to describe the weather. Write a place (town, city, country, or continent) where each type of weather is normal.

Page 90

THE COUNTRY
beach
forest
island
mountain
ocean
river
sky
town
tree
village

MOVE BEYOND
Are there any of these places where you live? Write their names.

OTHER IMPORTANT WORDS

audience	count	math	season	weather alert
autumn	day out	memory	snack	weather report
break	dollar	picnic	spring	winter
careful	dry season	rainy season	summer	working memory
cent	long-term memory	roller coaster	tip	
change				

IRREGULAR VERBS

base form	simple past	past participle
agree	agreed	agreed
be	was/were	been
break	broke	broken
bring	brought	brought
buy	bought	bought
can	could	been able to
choose	chose	chosen
come	came	come
cost	cost	cost
cut	cut	cut
do	did	done
draw	drew	drawn
drink	drank	drunk
drive	drove	driven
eat	ate	eaten
fall	fell	fallen
feel	felt	felt
find	found	found
fly	flew	flown
forget	forgot	forgotten
get	got	gotten
give	gave	given
go	went	gone
have	had	had
hear	heard	heard
hit	hit	hit
hurt	hurt	hurt
keep	kept	kept
know	knew	known
learn	learned	learned
let	let	let

base form	simple past	past participle
lie	lay	lain
make	made	made
meet	met	met
put	put	put
read	read	read
ride	rode	ridden
run	ran	run
say	said	said
see	saw	seen
send	sent	sent
set	set	set
shake	shook	shaken
show	showed	shown
sing	sang	sung
sit	sat	sat
sleep	slept	slept
speak	spoke	spoken
spend	spent	spent
stand	stood	stood
steal	stole	stolen
swim	swam	swum
take	took	taken
teach	taught	taught
tell	told	told
think	thought	thought
understand	understood	understood
wear	wore	worn
win	won	won
withdraw	withdrew	withdrawn
write	wrote	written

UNIT 2   LISTENING AND VOCABULARY

Page 24, Exercise 3

He has a big head, and he doesn't have any hair. He has one big red eye. His nose is blue. His mouth is very small, and he only has one tooth. He's doesn't have any arms. He has three legs and big feet.

UNIT 5   GRAMMAR

Page 57, Exercise 6

Choose one of the jobs and think of a person.

- A teacher
- An actor (male)
- A member of a pop group

UNIT 6   GRAMMAR

Page 67, Exercise 6

School trip A
San Francisco
Cost: $350
Days: four
Stay: in a small hotel
Activities: visit museums and famous buildings

UNIT 6   GRAMMAR

Page 69, Exercise 7

UNIT 7   GRAMMAR

Page 79, Exercise 7

Describe the picture of Bella's room to your partner. Don't look at your partner's picture. Find six differences.

ALL STUDENTS

UNIT 3   LISTENING AND VOCABULARY

Page 36, Exercise 5b

UNIT 2 LISTENING AND VOCABULARY

Page 24, Exercise 3

She has a small head and red hair. Her eyes are pink, and her face is green. She doesn't have a nose. She has big ears and a big mouth. Her teeth are yellow. She has one arm. She has two legs and four feet.

UNIT 5 GRAMMAR

Page 57, Exercise 6

Choose one of the jobs and think of a person.

- A famous soccer player
- An actor (female)
- A famous television cook
- A female member of a pop group

UNIT 6 GRAMMAR

Page 67, Exercise 6

School trip B
Movie studio
Cost: $190
Days: five
Stay: in tents
Activities: learn about movies, make a short movie

UNIT 6 GRAMMAR

Page 69, Exercise 7

UNIT 7 GRAMMAR

Page 79, Exercise 7

Describe the picture of Bella's room to your partner. Don't look at your partner's picture. Find six differences.

STEP-BY-STEP PROJECTS

Download more information from www.macmillangobeyond.com.

MAKE A COLLAGE

- Make a list of parts of the body – *hand, eyes, legs*.
- Find pictures of body parts in old magazines and newspapers.
- Cut out your pictures and make the collage.

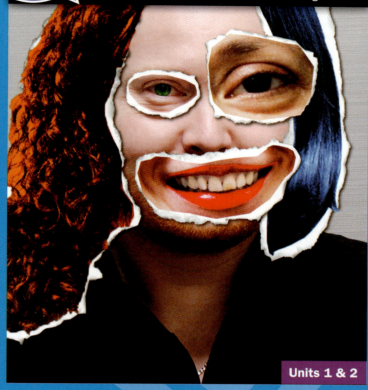

Units 1 & 2

DESIGN A DREAM HOME

- Choose a famous person to design the home for – *sports personality, movie star, singer*.
- List special things to include in the home – *gym, movie theater, studio*.
- Choose a location and design the home.

Units 5 & 6

PRESENT THE WEATHER

- Choose a location – *a country, a city, your local area*.
- Prepare the weather forecast. Include a report and sound effects.
- Present your weather report.

Units 7 & 8

FORM A BAND

- Choose a kind of band – *pop, hip-hop, rock*.
- Choose instruments to play – *drums, guitar, keyboard*.
- Give your band a name and write profiles for the band members.

Units 3 & 4

Macmillan Education
4 Crinan Street
London N1 9XW
A division of Springer Nature Limited

Companies and representatives throughout the world

ISBN 978-0-230-47292-1

Designed by EMC Design Ltd.

Illustrated by Seb Camagajevac (Beehive Illustration) p. 78; Peter Cornwell pp. 34, 35 (l), 36, 58 (girl with soccer ball), 115 (Unit 6 Grammar), 116 (Unit 6 Grammar); Tom Croft pp. 29, 48; Venitia Dean (Advocate-Art) p. 97; Sally Elford pp. 10 (music notes), 20 (people), 25, 32 (clock, coins, computer), 42 (cello, tv, books, CDs, shopping), 54 (menu, cash register, clock), 64 (onion, bed, bowl); 86 (banner artwork); Tony Forbes (Sylvie Poggio Artists) p. 15; Kev Hopgood pp. 23, 35 (r), 38, 44, 47, 67, 81, 84, 115 (Unit 3 Listening and Vocabulary); Bob Lea pp. 54–55; Caron Painter (Sylvie Poggio Artists) pp. 16, 19 (bottom), 21, 40, 85, 88, 115 (Unit 7 Grammar), 116 (Unit 7 Grammar); Zara Picken p. 24; Jamie Pogue (Bright Agency) pp. 6, 7, 8, 9; David Shephard (Bright Agency) p. 12; Tony Wilkins pp. 58, 86–87 (map).

Cover design by EMC Design Ltd.
Cover photograph by Alamy/Age Fotostock/Dennis MacDonald
Picture research by Tessa Hammond and Emily Taylor

The authors would like to thank all the team at Macmillan for everything they have done to make *Go Beyond* possible. We would like to thank Studio8 Ltd. and John Marshall Media, Inc. for their creative work on the videos, and the actors who bring the material to life. We would also like to thank John Marshall Media, Inc. for the production of the audio material. We'd also like to thank all the teachers and other individuals who have contributed to the course whose names appear on this page. A special thank you to Jade Todd and Jim Connolly for providing us with the wonderful free-time activity photos in Unit 4. Finally, we'd like thank our friends and families for all their support.

The authors and publishers would like to express thanks to all those who contributed to the development and formation of *Go Beyond*. In particular, we would like to thank the following teachers, contacts, and reviewers: Cristina Moisén Antón, Argelia Solis Arriaga, Krzysztof Bartold, Paweł Bienert, Agnieszka Bojanowska, Samuel Gómez Borobia, Ma. Eugenia Fernández Castro, Jolanta Chojnacka, Elsa Georgina Cruz, Dominika Dąbrowska, Barbara Dawidowska, Galina Dragunova, Monika Drygiel-Kobylińska, Mauricio Duran, Natalia Evdokimenko, Maria Teresa Velázquez Evers, Marciana Loma-Osorio Fontecha, Monika Fromiczew-Droździńska, Patricia García, Axel Morales García, Miguel Angel Rodriguez García, Aleksandra Gilewska, Joanna Góra, Ewa Górka, Daphne Green, Agata Helwich, Bethsabe Ruiz Herrera, Robert Jadachowski, Patricia Guzmán Luis Juan, Anna Kacpura, Ruth Kanter, Regina Kaźmierczuk, Katarzyna Konisiewicz, Maria Koprowska, Bogusława Krajewska, Aldona Krasoń, Joanna Worobiec Kugaj, Joanna Kuligowska, Tadeusz Kur, Maria Kwiatkowska, Josefina Maitret, Javier Majul, Claire Manners, Laura Elena Medina, Carmen García Méndez, Iwona Mikucka, Talhia Miranda, Claudia Rangel Miranda, Armando Nieto, Joanna Nowak, Anna Nowakowska, Ewa Nowicka, Anastasia Parshikova, Paloma Carrasco Peñalba, Ma. Del Carmen Fernández Pérez, Joanna Płatos, Louise Emma Potter, Maria Teresa Portillo, Juan José Gómez Ramírez, Aida Rivera, Gabriela Rubio, Gabriela Bourge Ruiz, Irina Sakharova, Małgorzata Sałaj, Patricia Avila Sánchez, Jessica Galvan Sanchez, Miguel Angel Santiago, Karol Sęk, Barbara Sibilska, Tatiana Sinyavina, Agnieszka Śliwowska, Vlada Songailene, Ángela Siles Suárez, Beata Świątkowska, Ewelina Szmyd-Patuła, Agnieszka Szymaniak, Juliana Maria Franco Tavares, José Luis Vázquez, Irma Velazquez, Małgorzata Walczak, Dariusz Winiarek, Justyna Zdunek, Zofia Żdżarska, Dominika Zięba, Marzena Zieleniewska, Anna Zielińska-Miszczuk, Robert Zielonka.

The authors and publishers would like to thank the following for permission to reproduce their images:

Alamy Used with permission from Microsoft p. 11(9), Alamy/42pix Premier p. 90(b), Alamy/AF archive p. 24(4), Alamy/Age Fotostock p. 70(tl), Alamy/All Star Photographs p. 24(3), Alamy/Arco Images pp. 32(b), 33(h), Alamy/Aurora Photos p. 65(br), Alamy/Big Cheese Photo LLC p. 25, Alamy/Richard G. Bingham II p. 37(tl), Alamy/John Birdsall p. 71, Alamy/blickwinkel p. 87(cr), Alamy/Built Images p. 64(c), Alamy/Thomas Cockrem p. 92(Maria), Alamy/Bea Cooper p. 64(cr), Alamy/Leila Cutler pp. 21(1), 22(Dan), Alamy/Darren Green Photography p. 86(tr), Alamy/EPA/Sergei Chirikov p. 87(tr), Alamy/Paul Fleet p. 81, Alamy/Betty Finney p. 65(tr, cm), Alamy/Viktor Fischer p. 13(6), Alamy/Foodfolio p. 69, Alamy/Patrick Forget/Sagaphoto p. 37(inset), Alamy/Eric Fowke p. 89(bm), Alamy/Clare Gainey p. 82(tr), Alamy/Bernardo Galmarini p. 86(cr),

Alamy/Bill Gozansky p. 65(cl), Alamy/Andrew Holt p. 62, Alamy/Doug Houghton p. 72(bl), Alamy/Huntstock Inc. p. 28(1), Alamy/imageBROKER pp. 27(bl), 32(a), 35, 90(c), Alamy/Image Source pp. 52, 64(cm), 82(cm), Alamy/Juniors Bildarchiv GmbH p. 33(j), Alamy/Kevers p. 12(br), Alamy/LOOK Die Bildagentur der Fotografen p. 90(a), Alamy/Oleksiy Maksymenko p. 117(tr), Alamy/Barry Mason p. 13(1), Alamy/Keith Morris p. 21(5), Alamy/Peter Adams Photography Ltd. p. 12(tr), Alamy/Thibaut PETIT-BARA p. 73(tr), Alamy/Peter Titmuss pp. 86(background), 87(br, background), Alamy/Picture Partners p. 26, Alamy/Radius Images p. 14(cr), Alamy/Andres Rodriguez p. 11(3), Alamy/Ed Rooney p. 82(background), Alamy/RTimages pp. 12(cm), 37(tr), Alamy/Mick Sinclair p. 82(cr), Alamy/Kumar Sriskandan p. 32(b), Alamy/StockbrokerXtra p. 91(br), Alamy/Top-Pet-Pics p. 34, Alamy/Renaud Visage p. 64(b);

BananaStock pp. 10(5), 11(12), 21(7), 70(tml);

Brand X Pictures p. 54(8);

Comstock p. 68(j);

Corbis p. 54(1,2,4), Corbis/Atlantide Phototravel p. 66(tr), Corbis/James Leynse p. 82(br), Corbis/Look Photography/Beateworks p. 17(br), Corbis/Marnie Burkhart p. 61, Corbis/Tom Martin/JAI p. 64(tr), Corbis/Ocean p. 45(tr), Corbis/Sebastian Pfuetze p. 21(9), Corbis/Grady Reese p. 70(tr), Corbis/Gregor Schuster p. 11(8), Corbis/Martin Siepmann/Westend61 p. 33(d), Corbis/Michael Zegers p. 66(Josina);

Creatas p. 11(14);

Digital Vision p. 68(k);

Getty Images pp. 10(10), 11(2), 56(cl), 68(h, l), 68(a,b), Getty Images/Alistair Berg p. 83(tr), Getty Images/Blend Images p. 93(cl), Getty Images/Peter Cade p. 79, Getty Images/Elisa Cicinelli p. 53(cr), Getty Images/Compassionate Eye Foundation/Robert Daly/OJO Images p. 60, Getty Images/Stewart Cohen p. 21(3), Getty Images/Cultura p. 21(2), Getty Images/Stuart Dee p. 24(1), Getty Images/Fuse p. 117(bl), Getty Images/ Petri Artturi Asikainen p. 91(tl), Getty Images/Judith Haeusler p. 49, Getty Images/Hiroshi Higuchi p. 96, Getty Images/Hill Street Studios p. 30, Getty Images/Neva MoAnik p. 28(3), Getty Images/National Geographic Creative p. 94, Getty Images/OJO Images p. 14(cl), Getty Images/Pixland p. 83(mr), Getty Images/Juan Silva p. 66(Ricardo), Getty Images/Tetra images RF p. 45(tl), Getty Images/Terraxplorer p. 64(a), Getty Images/Kerstin Waurick p. 53(cl), Getty Images/Westend61 p. 89(tl), Getty Images/Ziva_K p. 53(cm);

ImageSource pp. 22(Leo), 70(tmr), 83(br), 92(Jake);

iStock Images p. 13(tl);

Jupiter Images p. 19;

Macmillan Publishers Limited pp. 54(6), 68(g,i), Macmillan Publishers Limited/Paul Bricknell p. 23, Macmillan Publishers Limited/Sarah Greene p. 117(tl);

PhotoAlto p. 21(4);

PhotoDisc pp. 10(1), 32(c), PhotoDisc/Getty Images pp. 66(tml), 68(c, d);

Photoshot/Andia p. 24(2);

Plain Picture/PhotoAlto p. 18(cr), Plain Picture/Lumi Images/Romulic-Stojcic p. 56(tr);

Rex Features/Startraks Photo p. 24(5);

Stockbyte/PunchStock p. 67;

SuperStock pp. 33(g), Superstock/Blend Images p. 54(7);

ThinkStock pp. 11(4, 6, 7, 11, 13, 15), 54(3, 5), 68(e, f), 21(6), 22(Emma), 33(e,f), 39(tr), 44(boy, inset), 46(1,4,5), 50, 90(d), 92(Lucy), 93(tr, br), 117(cr), ThinkStock/Brand X Pictures p. 27(br), ThinkStock/Comstock Images p. 28(2), ThinkStock/Getty Images/Fuse p. 27(tr), 46(3), ThinkStock/Getty Images/Hemera pp. 33(i), 46(2), ThinkStock/Hemera Technologies p. 39(mr, br), ThinkStock/Getty Images/iStockphoto p. 13(2–5), 14(sunglasses), 17(cl), 18(cl, cm), ThinkStock/Jupiter Images p. 17(tr), ThinkStock/Moodboard p. 14(cm).

Commissioned photography by Jim Connolly and Jade Todd pp. 42–43; Studio 8 Ltd. pp. 76, 77, 80

These materials may contain links for third party websites. We have no control over, and are not responsible for, the contents of such third party websites. Please use care when accessing them.

Printed and bound in Spain
2022 2021 2020 2019 2018
14 13 12 11 10 9 8